The
DIVINE
COMFORTER

The DIVINE COMFORTER

The Person and Work of the Holy Spirit

J. DWIGHT PENTECOST

Grand Rapids, MI 49501

The Divine Comforter: The Person and Work of the Holy Spirit

Copyright © 1963 by J. Dwight Pentecost

Published in 1997 by Kregel Publications, a division of Kregel, Inc., P.O. Box 2607, Grand Rapids, MI 49501. Kregel Publications provides trusted, biblical publications for Christian growth and service. Your comments and suggestions are valued.

For more information about Kregel Publications, visit our web site at http://www.kregel.com.

Cover design: Sarah Slattery

Library of Congress Cataloging-in-Publication Data
Pentecost, J. Dwight.
    The divine Comforter: the person and work of the Holy Spirit / J. Dwight Pentecost.
        p.   cm.
    Originally published: Westwood, N.J.: Revell, © 1963.
Includes indexes.
    1. Holy Spirit. I. Title.
BT121.2.P4   1998   231'.3—dc21   97-30360
                                                    CIP

ISBN 0-8254-3456-4

Printed in the United States of America

2 3 / 03 02 01 00 99 98

To my daughters
JANE and GWENDOLYN
this volume is dedicated
with love

CONTENTS

PREFACE

IN A DAY WHEN THE WORLD HAS BECOME POWER CONSCIOUS, little is known of the divine power available to the child of God through the Divine Comforter who was promised by the Lord Jesus Christ to His disciples before his death, resurrection and ascension. He said, "I will pray the Father, and he shall give you another Comforter, that he may abide with you for ever" (John 14:16). "It is expedient for you that I go away: for if I go not away, the Comforter will not come unto you; but if I depart, I will send him unto you" (John 16:7).

It is our purpose to present, through these studies in the Person and work of the Holy Spirit, the "exceeding greatness of his power to us-ward who believe . . ." (Ephesians 1:19), a power that is available to God's children because the promised Comforter has been sent by the ascended and glorified Christ.

These studies were first presented to the congregation of Grace Bible Church of Dallas, Texas, of which the author is pastor. Deep and abiding appreciation is expressed to Mrs. Paul Allen and Mrs. Offie Bayless for their tireless work in transcribing tapes and preparing manuscripts for editing and publication. Without their ministry, rendered as unto the Lord, this volume would not have been possible. These studies are now sent forth to a wider congregation with the prayer that the Holy Spirit, whose ministry it is to lead us into all truth, might lead the readers into a fuller knowledge of His Person and His work.

J. DWIGHT PENTECOST

Dallas, Texas

1

THE SPIRIT: A PERSON
OR AN INFLUENCE

IF I WERE TO ASK YOU, "IS JESUS CHRIST A PERSON, AND ARE YOU
conscious of personal fellowship with Him?" without doubt
or hesitation you would reply, "Of course, He is very real to
me." If I were to ask you, "Is God the Father a Person,
and are you conscious of personal fellowship with Him?"
with perhaps a little less assurance you would respond, "Yes,
I know God is a Person, and even though I feel closer to
and more intimately associated with the Lord Jesus Christ,
I recognize that fellowship with God the Father is possible."
If I were to ask you, "Is the Holy Spirit a Person, and are
you conscious of personal relationship with Him?" proba-
ably you would say, "I have never been conscious of any personal fellowship with the Holy Spirit," or, "How can you
have fellowship with the Holy Ghost?"

As we present to you the teaching that the Holy Spirit is
a Person, you may feel that the subject under consideration
is best reserved for a theological classroom. However, no subsequent study in the great doctrines of the work of the Holy
Spirit will mean much to you personally unless you realize
that we are considering One who is as much a Person as God
the Father or God the Son. The Holy Spirit is as much a
Person as you are or I am.

As we study these important doctrines, it is not our desire

only to enlighten your mind so that you might grasp the truth of the Word intellectually; it is our desire to bring you face to face with a Person so that you might enjoy fellowship with Him. A person can only have fellowship with another person. Therefore we begin our study of the ministry of the Holy Spirit with a consideration of the question, "Is the Holy Spirit a Person or an influence?" so that you may know He possesses all the components of personality. We may fellowship with Him, listen to Him speak, love Him and obey Him.

Several centuries after the death of Christ, there lived a man who became known for his heretical views. His name was Arius. He said that the Holy Spirit was only the exerted energy of God: Since God the Father is a person, His personality may manifest itself, and that manifestation of the personality of the Father is the exercised energy that goes forth from the Father. Arius therefore denied the true personality of the third person of the Trinity, the Holy Spirit. While that interpretation was condemned at the Council of Nicea in A.D. 325 as an heretical interpretation and an heretical doctrine, it did not cease. Following the Reformation, Socinus took up the condemned heresy of Arius. He denied the personality of the Holy Spirit, and took one further step by saying that the Spirit is the *eternally* proceeding energy of God: Since God is eternal, and God as a Person was always manifesting power, that eternal manifestation of the power of God was the Spirit of God. This doctrine has come to be the foundation of Unitarianism and those kindred movements which deny the Trinity. It is an interpretation which the Word of God condemns and which the church in its past history has held to be an heretical doctrine.

What, then, is the basis of this concept that the Holy Spirit is an influence or a power or energy, and not a Person?

It is based chiefly on the fact that the Greek word that is translated "spirit" is neuter in gender. It is the Greek word *pneuma,* the word for "spirit" or "air." You are familiar with it in our English word "pneumatic": you ride on pneumatic tires, tires that are inflated with *pneuma,* or air or breath. Because the word *pneuma* is neuter, translators of the Bible sometimes translated the pronoun that referred to the Spirit as "it." Romans 8:26 reads: "the Spirit *itself* maketh intercession for us. . . ." Because of that accident of English translation, many have thought that the Holy Spirit is not "He," but "it." That which is "it" is not a person. It is from that translation that a great deal of false doctrine has derived.

Now we find a strange thing in connection with the translation of the original text. Even though the word "spirit," or *pneuma,* is neuter, there are occasions where the masculine pronoun is used. In John 14:26 we read: "But the Comforter, which is the Holy Ghost, whom the Father will send you in my name, *he* [that is, the Holy Spirit] shall teach you all things. . . ." The only reason that the Greek text could use the masculine pronoun "he," when it refers to the neuter noun *pneuma* or "spirit," was because it was recognized that the Spirit was not an influence or a power, but a Person. Therefore this masculine pronoun must be used in reference to the Spirit. We find the same thing again in John 16:13-14: "Howbeit when he, the Spirit of truth, is come, he will guide you into all truth: for he shall not speak of himself; but whatsoever he shall hear, that shall he speak: and he will shew you things to come." For many of you this may seem to be a technicality and of relative unimportance, yet it is a very important consideration. From the original text itself, we see that because *pneuma,* or the spirit, happened to be a neuter noun, one may not infer that the Holy Spirit is not a Person.

Let us examine several passages of Scripture that show us quite conclusively that the Holy Spirit is, first of all, a Person, and second, that the Holy Spirit is God. We usually divide the categories of personality into three realms: intellect, emotion and will. With the intellect a person can know and think and understand. With the emotional capacity, a person can feel and love. With the will, a person can decide and act. You can prove that you are a person because you think, because you love, and because you will certain things into action. If we can see, from the Word of God, that the Holy Spirit has these capacities, we would have to conclude that He is a Person.

In I Corinthians 2:10-11 we have a ministry of the Spirit that reveals His capacity of intellect. Paul tells us, "God hath revealed them unto us by his Spirit: for the Spirit searcheth all things, yea, the deep things of God. For what man knoweth the things of man, save the spirit of man which is in him? even so the things of God knoweth no man, but the Spirit of God." The Spirit of God *knoweth*. Now, what does the Spirit of God know? He knows the deep things of God. All that is in the Father, and all that repository of divine truth that is in the Father, is understood and known by the Holy Spirit. Because He knows, He can reveal what He knows concerning God. It is difficult for a man to teach something that he doesn't know himself, and one of the first requisites of a good teacher is that he must know his subject. If the Holy Spirit is able to teach the things of Christ, reveal the things of the Father and the Son, it is because He knows the things of God. And the Spirit knows because He possesses the capacity of intellect, the ability to know—one of the necessary components of a true personality.

In Ephesians 4:30 we have a clue to the emotional capacity

of the Holy Spirit: "grieve not the holy Spirit of God, whereby ye are sealed unto the day of redemption." Grief is a manifestation of the capacity of emotion, and a person must have the ability to love before love can be grieved. The fact that the Holy Spirit can be grieved is revelation that the Spirit possesses an emotional capacity, which may be wounded by sins against His heart. Hence, as the Apostle gives us the command, "grieve not the holy Spirit," indirectly he is teaching us the fact that the Holy Spirit possesses the capacity of emotion.

In I Corinthians 12 the Apostle is teaching us about spiritual gifts, and in verse 11 Paul writes, "But all these worketh that one and selfsame Spirit, dividing to every man severally [individually] as he will." Here the Apostle says that the distribution of spiritual gifts is the result of an act of the will of the Holy Spirit of God. Paul clearly attributes to the Holy Spirit the capacity of will. When we put these three passages together, we observe that the Holy Spirit possesses the capacity of intellect, so that He can know; the capacity of emotion, so that He can love and His love can be sinned against; and the capacity of will, so that He can decide and bring action into being. Because of this we would say that the Holy Spirit is not an influence, not a power emanating from God, nor a manifestation of God's personality; but the Holy Spirit is a Person as much as you are a person, and the same proofs of your personality are demonstrable concerning the Holy Spirit of God.

Is the Holy Spirit God? Is the Holy Spirit Deity? The Word of God presents the truth that the Spirit, no less than the Father and the Son, is God, and all three are one in essence, one in being, one in their attributes. The Word of God relates the Holy Spirit to both the Father and the Son.

And since they are related to each other and equated with each other, on the basis of the principle that two things equal to the same thing are equal to each other, we must conclude that the Spirit is Deity.

Several passages show the relationship of the Holy Spirit to God the Father. In Matthew 3:16 we read, "And Jesus, when he was baptized, went up straightway out of the water: and, lo, the heavens were opened unto him, and he saw the Spirit of God descending like a dove, and lighting upon him." Here the Holy Spirit is called "the Spirit of God," stressing the equality of the Spirit with the Father. In Luke 4:18 we find that He is referred to as "The Spirit of the Lord. . . ." In Isaiah 61:1 He is referred to as "The Spirit of the Lord God. . . ." There are many other references that could be given to relate the Spirit to the Father, but these three are sufficient to show that the Word of God relates Him to God the Father, for He is the Spirit of God, the Spirit of the Lord, or the Spirit of the Lord God.

Not only is the Spirit related to the Father, but He is also related to the Son. In Romans 8:9 Paul writes, "But ye are not in the flesh, but in the Spirit, if so be that the Spirit of God dwell in you. Now if any man have not the Spirit of Christ, he is none of his." In the beginning of that verse Paul refers to the Spirit of God and then, in the next phrase, he refers to the Spirit of Christ. The Spirit, who is related to God, is also related to Christ, for He is "the Spirit of Christ." The Apostle, in Philippians 1:19, says, "I know that this shall turn to my salvation through your prayer, and the supply of the Spirit of Jesus Christ." The fact that the Spirit is related to the Father establishes His Deity; the fact that He is related to the Son is added substantiation of His Deity.

The titles used to refer to the Holy Spirit show us that He

possesses the same attributes that God the Father and God the Son possess. The Holy Spirit, if He is God, cannot be less than God. There must be in the Spirit that which is in the Father and in the Son. In Hebrews 9:14 we read, "How much more shall the blood of Christ, who through the eternal Spirit offered himself without spot to God, purge your conscience from dead works to serve the living God?" There are different interpretations given to this verse, and particularly this phrase, "the eternal Spirit." Some see this as a reference to the eternal spirit of the Lord Jesus Christ; there are others who are quite satisfied that the eternal Spirit is a reference to the third Person of the Trinity and that He is referred to in the same way God the Father and God the Son are referred to; He is the eternal One. If the Spirit of God possesses the eternalness of God, it therefore is evident that He is equal with God and possesses full Deity.

In Romans 8:2 the Apostle refers to life possessed by the Spirit: "For the law of the Spirit of life in Christ Jesus hath made me free from the law of sin and death." The Spirit is the living One. As the living One, He possesses the same life that God possesses. God does not possess created life; God possesses uncreated life. Created life had its beginning in time; uncreated life is eternal life. The Spirit of God possesses the same quality of life that God the Father possesses. When He is referred to as the Spirit of life, it is not only a reference to the fact that He *gives* life, but that He *is* life.

In Romans 1:4 the Spirit is referred to as "the spirit of holiness." The Spirit of God, no less than God the Father and God the Son, possesses unchangeable, unalterable holiness. That quality of holiness belonging to God the Father and Son likewise belongs to the Holy Spirit, and we refer to Him as He is referred to all through the Word of God as the Holy

Spirit. That says more than that the Spirit does not commit any sin, or that He has never sinned. While that is true, this title, the Holy Spirit, emphasizes for us the fact of the oneness of the essence of the Spirit with the essence of God. A Holy God, a Holy Son and a Holy Spirit; three in one.

In John 14:17 we observe that the Spirit is "the Spirit of Truth." This says more than that the Holy Spirit tells us true things. Rather it affirms that the Holy Spirit, in His being, *is* Truth, and that, as Truth, He can reveal truth to man. This further attests the equality of the Spirit with the Father and the Son.

God is omnipotent, omniscient and omnipresent. Those words of course, are Latin derivatives which simply mean that God is all-powerful, God is all-wise and God is everywhere present. As we go into the Scripture, we observe that the Holy Spirit is said to be omnipotent, omniscient and omnipresent. The omnipotence of the Spirit is affirmed in Genesis 1:12 where, concerning the act of creation, we read: "In the beginning God created the heaven and the earth," and then, "the earth was without form, and void; and darkness was upon the face of the deep. And the Spirit of God [that is, the third Person of the Trinity] moved upon the face of the waters." The Holy Spirit was an active agent in the creation of all things. When we look at the vast expanse of this universe, we recognize that God the Father was the Architect and Jesus Christ was the Builder, for "All things were made by him; and without him was not any thing made that was made" (John 1:3). The Holy Spirit was the active agent in creation. Thus Genesis 1:2 demonstrates the omnipotence of the Spirit of God, for He brooded upon the face of the waters and creation came into existence because of the operation of the Spirit of God.

There is a greater demonstration of the omnipotence of the Spirit of God than that shown in creation and that is the omnipotence that was manifested by the Spirit in the salvation of your soul. The Spirt of God moved upon that which was dead, devoid of spiritual life and at enmity with God, that which was lawless and rebellious and stubborn. And the Spirit of God manifested omnipotence as He brought life out of that which was dead and caused the enmity to be turned to amity and brought one who was a child of the evil one into the family of God as His own child by faith in the Lord Jesus Christ. The Holy Spirit is God for He possesses the omnipotence of God.

There are no secrets that God the Father has from God the Holy Spirit, and the deep things of God are known to Him. Likewise, there is no secret locked away in the recesses of your heart or mine that is unknown to the Spirit of God. He knows every thought and intent of the heart. He is the omniscient one.

When we think of the omnipresence of the Spirit of God, we could go into a passage such as David penned in Psalm 139:7-10: "Whither shall I go from thy spirit? or whither shall I flee from thy presence? If I ascend up into heaven, thou art there: if I make my bed in hell, behold, thou art there. If I take the wings of the morning, and dwell in the uttermost parts of the sea; Even there shall thy hand lead me, and thy right hand shall hold me." And there the omnipresence of the Father and the Spirit are affirmed by the psalmist. "Whither shall I go from thy spirit?" The Holy Spirit, no less than the Father, is omnipresent.

It is the consistent teaching of the Word of God that the Holy Spirit is a Person. This Person dwells within all believers: "your body is the temple of the Holy Ghost . . ."

(I Corinthians 6:19). It is not some impersonal influence or force that has moved into you. It is a Person who has moved in and clothed Himself with your body. Therefore, personal, intimate fellowship is possible between you and the Holy Spirit. As a Person He wants to be known and wants to cause you to know Him. He wants to love and He wants to be loved. He has a will and He wants His will to be followed and obeyed. If we are indwelt with only a power, the question is, "How can power be released through the individual?" But the Christian life is more than a manifestation of some impersonal power through the individual; it is the manifestation of a Person. God's purpose in redemption is to bring believers into fellowship with Himself. Therefore, He has given believers a mind to know Him, a heart to love Him, a will to obey Him. He has put a Person within, with whom the believer can have the most personal intimate relationship. At the incarnation the Son of God came to tabernacle among men. On the day of Pentecost the Spirit of God came to tabernacle in men who believe. Not an influence, not a power, but a Person has come!

2

THE SPIRIT AND THE
REVELATION OF DIVINE TRUTH

A PHILOSOPHER IS A MAN WHO TELLS US WHAT HE THINKS. A scientist is a man who tells us what he knows or has discovered. A gossip is one who tells us what he suspects. But a witness is one who tells us what he has seen and heard. Before one can give a revelation of fact, one must know that fact, and apart from an experimental entrance into any truth, it is impossible for an individual to impart truth to another person. We are to consider a very important subject in reference to the Person and work of the Holy Spirit: the Holy Spirit as the revealer of truth; the Holy Spirit and His relationship to divine revelation.

The Apostle writes, "Eye hath not seen, nor ear heard, neither have entered into the heart of man, the things which God hath prepared for them that love him. But God hath revealed them unto us by his Spirit . . ." (I Corinthians 2:9-10). The Holy Spirit is the agent in divine revelation and that which is incomprehensible and undiscoverable to the natural mind has been revealed to us by Him. This same passage tells us the reason that the Holy Spirit is able to reveal truth: "for the Spirit searcheth all things, yea, the deep things of God. For what man knoweth the things of a man, save the spirit of man which is in him? even so the things of God knoweth no man, but the Spirit of God" (vv. 10-11).

Because the Spirit of God is one with the Father and the Son, the Spirit discerns and understands the deep things of God and is able to reveal them to man.

Natural men may discover things that are true but they cannot discover truth, for truth is not in things but in a Person. God is the source of all truth and men know truth only as they know God. So the Holy Spirit has come in order that He might be the revealer of divine truth to men who are in ignorance. It is a very humbling fact to have to acknowledge our ignorance. It is difficult to say, "I don't know." It is especially difficult to confess ignorance when a fact has been presented and we are supposed to know that fact. Men, by their own unaided intelligence, cannot fathom the truth of the Word of God, and the Holy Spirit has come to do a work of revealing. To reveal a truth is to set that truth openly before us so that we may understand it and enter into it. The Holy Spirit has come to display the truth of God; He has come to make a Person known, so that as we come to know Him who is the Way, the Truth and the Life, we might know the truth of God.

Consider several references in different portions of the Word of God so that you may see that the revelation of truth is the ministry of the Spirit. In the Old Testament poetical Books the Spirit was the revealer. In II Samuel 23:2 David said, "The Spirit of the Lord spake by me, and his word was in my tongue." You will notice in 23:1 that David is referred to as "the anointed of the God of Jacob, and the sweet psalmist of Israel." But David says that it was not his own word which he was putting into his psalms. The songs that he sang to the praise of God were not of his own origination, but rather it was the Spirit of the Lord who spoke through David and the Spirit's word "was in my tongue." David was so possessed and controlled by the Spirit of God that He made a revelation to David: The Word was not David's but the Spirit's. We find that the statement recorded here in II Samuel 23 would have reference to all of that portion of the Word of God that we know as the poetical Books.

In Ezekiel 2:2 the prophet says, "the spirit entered into me when he spake unto me, and set me upon my feet, that I heard him that spake unto me." A message was delivered to Ezekiel which he was able to hear and record. The word was not Ezekiel's; it was a word revealed to the prophet, and then through the prophet to the nation Israel. That which was given to us in Ezekiel 2:2 would likewise be true of all the prophetic portion of the Word of God.

In the Book of Exodus we find that Moses adds his testimony to the fact that the Spirit was the revealer of divine truth. In Exodus 19:9 the Lord said unto Moses, "Lo, I come unto thee in a thick cloud, that the people may hear when I speak with thee, and believe thee for ever." And then, in 20:1, we read: "God spake all these words, saying." All that Moses wrote in the Pentateuch he wrote because truth had been revealed to him. Thus we observe that each section of the Old Testament, the law, the prophets and the writings, were revelations by the Spirit of God to those who were instruments in passing on that revelation to us.

Consider the prophecy of Micah, who was contrasted with the false prophets who were speaking to Israel: "Thus saith the Lord concerning the prophets that make my people err, that bite with their teeth, and cry, Peace; and he that putteth not into their mouths, they even prepare war against him. Therefore night shall be unto you, that ye shall not have a vision; and it shall be dark unto you, that ye shall not divine; and the sun shall go down over the prophets, and the day shall be dark over them. Then shall the seers be ashamed, and the diviners confounded: yea, they shall all cover their lips; for there is no answer of God" (Micah 3:5-7). False prophets had arisen in Micah's day and they had gained the ears of the people. When the true prophets announced divine judgment because of apostasy and idolatry, false prophets arose and said they had a revelation from God that there would be no divine judgment. But God said these false prophets were to wander as men in darkness; when they looked for a vision, there would be none; when they looked for light to give to the people, there would be none. But in contrast to these false prophets the prophet Micah speaks: "But truly I am full of power by the spirit of the Lord . . ." (3:8). Whereas there was ignorance and blindness and darkness in the false prophets, Micah was full of power that had come by the Spirit of the Lord, so that he was able to speak authoritatively "to declare unto Jacob his transgression, and to Israel his sin" (3:8). The prophet Micah had a message to give to the people because the Spirit of the Lord had revealed truth to him.

We find in a passage such as Acts 1:16 that the New Testament also recognizes that the revelation of truth is the work of the Holy Spirit. The Apostles are gathered in the upper room and Peter says, "Men and brethren, this scripture must needs have been fulfilled, which the Holy Ghost by the mouth of David spake before concerning Judas. . . ." The prophecy of David the Psalmist is said to be the work of the Holy Spirit, so that the truth concerning the betrayal by Judas, which could never have been known by David, was revealed to David by the Holy Spirit, the revealer of truth.

We see this same truth given in the Epistle to the Hebrews 9:6-7. The Apostle writes concerning the Old Testament order of the priests, the tabernacle and the service of God.

But he tells us that "The Holy Ghost this signifying, that the way into the holiest of all was not yet made manifest, while as the first tabernacle was yet standing" v. 8. The writer states that the Holy Spirit was revealing truth through the tabernacle and that it was the Spirit who originated the truth that was understood. After quoting the Old Testament, the writer says, "Whereof the Holy Ghost also is a witness to us: for after that he had said before, This is the covenant . . ." (10:15-16). It is the Holy Spirit who was a *witness* and the Spirit passed on that which he had seen and known in revelation.

Perhaps the passage in II Peter 1:15-21 is the clearest New Testament passage showing us that the Spirit of God is the revealer of truth. In this letter the Apostle is exercising a pastoral ministry: he is writing to those who have been scattered abroad, who have heard the word of truth, but who, because they are scattered, do not have one upon whom they can depend for instruction. So Peter writes to teach them. He tells them that he is anticipating his death at any time but that he has made provision so that after he is gone, men can still know the truth: "I will endeavour that ye may be able after my decease to have these things always in remembrance" (v.15). Peter was reducing truth to writing and he authenticates his message and certifies the trustworthiness of the message which he has delivered by referring to the experience that he had when he was in the mountains with the Lord Jesus Christ, where God the Father testified to the honor and the glory that belonged to Jesus Christ and revealed the glory of Christ at His second coming. It was God the Father who revealed truth to the disciples concerning the Person and the work of Jesus Christ on the Mount of Transfiguration. We would agree that when the Father speaks there is an incontrovertible revelation of truth. Peter simply recorded the truth that he had heard from the Father. He testified to the fact that he had not followed a cunningly made-up tale, but simply recorded what had been revealed.

But now Peter says, "We have also a more sure word of prophecy . . ." (v.19). More sure than what? "Why, more sure word than the testimony I gave to you concerning the Father's revelation!" This is a remarkable statement. Remember that Peter was a witness and there were others with Peter who were witnesses. They had heard the Father speak and all could testify to what the Father said. What is this "more sure word of prophecy?" "Knowing this first, that no prophecy of the scripture is of any *private* interpretation" (v. 20). We are suffering from a poor translation here and consequently the truth that Peter is trying to get across to us has been obscured. A variant reading is: "Knowing this first, that no prophecy of scripture is of *its own* interpretation." That is, no passage is isolated from all that the Word has given elsewhere. That certainly is true, but that is not what Peter is writing, for he is not dealing with the interpretation of Scripture, but rather with the origin of Scripture. Peter says you have a more sure word of prophecy, "knowing this, that no prophecy of the Scripture is of its own *origination.*" That is, prophecy did not originate in the mind of the author who did the writing. Rather, "prophecy came not in old time by the will of man: but holy men of God spake as they were moved [that is, borne along as the wind bears along a sailboat] by the Holy Ghost" (v. 21). In these verses, then, the Apostle is speaking not so much of *inspiration* as of *revelation.* Scripture did not originate with men, but with the Revealer who knew the truth of God and revealed that truth to men. It was to be recorded so that we would possess the truth after those who wrote had gone home to be with the Lord.

Peter is teaching us that God is truth, and that men do not know the truth of God. If men are to know truth, it must be revealed. If the Scriptures originated in the minds of men, we have nothing but a record of man's search for God, and this world is filled with the rationalization of natural men who are trying to think their way to God. Since this Book did not originate with men, but was rather a revelation to men, we have the truth of God in the Word, because no Scripture is of its own *origination*. Holy men of God spoke as they were borne along in the reception of truth by the Revealer Himself.

It may have escaped your attention that the Spirit of God has used many different methods to reveal truth to men. The first method is revelation by a spoken word. In the Old and the New Testaments you frequently find the expression, "thus saith the Lord." In Acts 1:16 Peter says that the One speaking in the Old Testament was the Holy Spirit. In the Old Testament the Speaker seems to have been God. In Exodus 19:9-20:1 Moses was able to write down the very words which he heard God speak, and he recognized that this was a divine revelation. One of the plainest passages to support it is found in I Samuel 3. The child Samuel was awakened at night and he heard a voice speaking to him, calling, "Samuel" (v. 4). He ran to Eli and said, "Here am I" (v. 5). What does that show us? God was speaking with a voice that sounded so like the voice of a man that a child could not tell the difference. When Samuel discovered that it was the Lord speaking he said, "Speak; for thy servant heareth" (v. 10). God made a revelation to him in spoken words so that Samuel understood the judgment that was to come upon the house of Eli.

In the Book of Genesis revelation frequently was made

through dreams. As early as Genesis 20, Abimelech was warned in a dream that Sarah was not to be taken as his wife because she belonged to another man. In Genesis 28:11-12, when Jacob was fleeing after he had stolen the blessing, we read that he had lain down to sleep and he "dreamed, and behold a ladder [was] set up. . . ." Out of that dream came a revelation and a promise as God said, "I am the Lord God of Abraham thy father, and the God of Isaac: the land whereon thy liest, to thee will I give it, and to thy seed" (v. 13). Then "Jacob awaked out of his sleep, and he said, Surely the Lord is in this place; and I knew it not" (v. 16).

Another very familiar instance of a dream occurs in Genesis 37 when Joseph had a dream that got him into trouble because he didn't keep it to himself. It was revealed in the dream that he would be exalted and his brothers would bow down before him. He wound up in a pit and later was taken to Egypt before the revelation given to him in a dream was fulfilled. In the prophecy of Daniel, the dream of Nebuchadnezzar (2:31-45) gives the course of Gentile world-empire, and the four great beasts in Daniel's dream (7:2-27) reveal the prophetic program for the Gentiles.

The third method is revelation through visions. Isaiah the prophet says, "The vision of Isaiah the son of Amoz, which he saw concerning Judah and Jerusalem . . ." (1:1). In 6:1 we read: "In the year that King Uzziah died I saw also the Lord sitting upon a throne, high and lifted up, and his train filled the temple." In Ezekiel 1:3 we learn that Ezekiel was given a vision. Many more instances could be cited in the Old Testament. Or you can turn to the New Testament, in Acts 10, where we have the interesting record of what took place in the house of Cornelius. Cornelius was a devout man, "one that feared God with all his house . . ." (v. 2). "He saw in a vision . . . an angel of God coming in to him, and saying unto him, Cornelius" (v. 3). A revelation was made to Cornelius that he was to send for Peter. According to Revelation I, John, on the Isle of Patmos, was in the Spirit on the Lord's day, and he *saw* the Lord in His transcendent excellence.

The difference between revelation in a dream and revelation through a vision is simply the difference between being asleep and being awake when the revelation is made. In the dream the recipient was in the state of sleep; in the vision he was in a waking state when God revealed a certain truth.

Another method of revealing truth was through trances. In Acts 10 we find that God was working with Peter in preparation for sending the gospel to Cornelius: Peter "went up upon the housetop to pray about the sixth hour: And he became very hungry, and would have eaten: but while they made ready, he fell into a trance, And saw heaven opened . . ." (10:9-11). God revealed to Peter through this trance the great truth that Gentiles were acceptable to Him.

The first six chapters of Zechariah are another outstanding example of this method of revelation. The prophet Zechariah was in a trance when God made revelation to him concerning the ages of Israel's history. Now the difference between the trance and the vision is that in the vision the recipient received revelation through his own faculties of perception, but in the trance the recipient of revelation was lifted out of himself into a state of supernatural hearing, seeing and acting. Zechariah was like an actor in all of the revelations that God made to him. He stood there, he performed certain acts, he asked questions, he entered into discussions with the revealing angel as well as with God; but he was in a state of supernatural hearing and seeing.

We have seen that sometimes revelation was made through the spoken Word, but with great frequency, particularly in the Old Testament, revelation of truth was given through dreams or visions or trances. God does not use these methods today for the simple reason that revelation has been completed through the Person of Jesus Christ and through the inspiration of the Scriptures. Those who have the Word of God, and those who have received Jesus Christ and the revelations which He gives, have all the truth that God has to reveal to man. Men who are still looking for added revelation through visions and dreams and trances are saying, in effect, that God has not made sufficient revelation. Soothsayers, astrologers, fortunetellers, and the rest of their ilk, attract a great following for they profess to be able to reveal truth by interpretation of various symbols. These are a demonic imitation of the method which the Spirit of God used to reveal divine truth.

There is one more facet of this subject which we should consider briefly. In John 14:16 we read that the Spirit of God will reveal truth to the children of God as He reveals a person and as He opens up the Word. In John 14:26 we read, "But the Comforter, which is the Holy Ghost, whom the Father will send in my name, we shall teach you all things, and bring all things to your remembrance, whatsoever I have said unto you." Jesus Christ is giving a word of instruction to His disciples. He has professed in John 14:6 to be the truth. He has also spoken the truth of God. His words are truth. When He will be absent from them, He will not be able to cause them to understand the truth that He has revealed. The disciples, even after three years of instruction at the feet of Jesus Christ, were still ignorant of God's revealed truth. The Lord had spoken to them but they had not understood Him. They need

One who will enlighten them; they need One who will illumine that which has been spoken and that which will yet be written. Our Lord here promises that the Holy Spirit, whom the Father will send, "shall teach you all things, and bring all things to your remembrance, whatsoever *I* have said unto you." Observe that the Holy Spirit has not been promised to teach us anything other than what Jesus Christ has said. It has not been promised that He will teach theology, or Greek, or church history. It has not been promised He will teach history or chemistry or physics or any other subject. But it has been promised that He will "teach you all things, and bring all things . . . whatsoever I have said unto you." The subject matter of His teaching is circumscribed and limited.

In John 16:12 our Lord is continuing the same theme as He says, "I have yet many things to say unto you, but ye cannot bear them now." Because the disciples were ignorant of the basic fact of the death and resurrection of Christ, they were incapable of receiving and understanding truth. Even though it had been openly set before them by the Lord Jesus Christ, they were unable to appropriate it. The Lord had to say, "Howbeit when he, the Spirit of truth, is come, he will guide you into all truth: for he shall not speak of himself; but whatsoever he shall hear, that shall he speak: and he will shew you things to come. He shall glorify me: for he shall receive of mine, and shall shew it unto you" (16:13-14). When our Lord said that "he will shew you things to come," He was not speaking of prophecy. He was not saying that the Holy Spirit would reveal, or cause them to understand, future things. This is a reference to the Spirit's relationship to the Scriptures which had not yet been written at the time that the Lord spoke, but which would be written. When the

Lord spoke these words, not one of the four Gospels had been written; the Book of Acts had not been written; not one of the Epistles of the New Testament had been written; the Book of the Revelation had not been written; there was not a single line of New Testament Scripture written. How was the Holy Spirit to teach the disciples the revealed truth of God? Before the disciples passed from the scene they would bear witness to the truth that they had seen. How would succeeding generations know the truth that God had revealed? Why, the Holy Spirit will show the things to come; the Holy Spirit would continue His revelation of truth so that the New Testament could be written. The New Testament did not originate in the minds of men, but holy men of God spoke it as they were borne along by the Holy Spirit. Therefore, the whole New Testament is the fulfillment of our Lord's promise that the Spirit, who came to make revelation, would show the things to come.

The Holy Spirit will also interpret to us that which He caused to be written. When one teaches the Word of God faithfully, and we come to understand truth concerning God through this teacher, it is actually the Holy Spirit doing His work of causing us to understand the Scriptures, as our Lord promised. The Holy Spirit, then, is an illuminator. He does not reveal new truth today; we do not discover new things about God. We can only come to understand what had already been revealed by the Holy Spirit. We do not ask God for revelation; we ask God for illumination that we might understand the revelation that has already been given.

Think of our Lord walking with the two disciples on the way to Emmaus. He took the Old Testament Scriptures and went through them book by book, teaching them things concerning Himself. As He unfolded the Old Testament, Jesus

Christ was doing the work of illuminating the Old Testament to cause them to understand what had been written. The Lord Jesus *walked alongside* of those two, doing the work of illumination. But the Holy Spirit *dwells within* us that He might cause the light of His knowledge to be shed abroad in our hearts.

"He shall glorify me," our Lord said, "for he shall receive of mine, and shall shew it unto you" (John 16:14). The Holy Spirit doesn't teach just for the joy of teaching. The Holy Spirit teaches to reveal a Person. This is teaching with a purpose. Our Lord said, "I, if I be lifted up . . . , will draw all men unto me" (John 12:32). And Jesus Christ was lifted up from the tomb, exalted by God, the Father. The Holy Spirit has been given the ministry of drawing men unto the One who has been lifted up. The Holy Spirit has taken on the work of giving revelation and causing men to understand the revelation so that Jesus Christ might be exalted as the preeminent One.

I think it significant that in the Word of God we have over two hundred names and titles applied to the Lord Jesus Christ, but when we come to the third Person of the Trinity, the Holy Spirit who does the work of revealing, He is primarily referred to as the Spirit, or the Holy Spirit, or the Spirit of God. No long list of names and titles are used concerning the One who is as much God as the Father or the Son. Why? Because His ministry is not to glorify Himself, but our Lord Jesus. We have a revelation of the truth of God, and that truth centers in a Person, the Lord Jesus Christ. The revelation of God for men has been recorded by the Spirit's work in the written Word. The Spirit will take the written Word, His revelation, and cause us to understand it so that it might be the means of bringing us into an intimate knowledge of the One who is the Truth of God. We are to search the Scriptures, not to receive knowledge, not to gain facts, not to be teachers or expounders of the Word; but we are to study the Scriptures under the Spirit's guidance that we might come to know a Person. Knowing Him we know the truth of God.

3

THE SPIRIT AND THE INSPIRATION OF SCRIPTURE

THE WORD OF GOD MAKES CLAIMS FOR ITSELF WHICH, IF THEY be true, cause us to revere every word that has been written. If they be false, we must logically reject the Word of God in its entirety. The Bible asserts that it is no ordinary book, but that it is the Word of God. It claims to have the authority and power of the Spirit of God Himself. The Word of God affirms that it is living and powerful, sharper than any two-edged sword, and that it can pierce even to the depths of the soul and the spirit. If the Word of God is given to us by inspiration of God, then we must listen to it, we must know it, we must believe it, and we must obey it. But if a book claims to have come directly from God to reveal the truth of God to us, and purports to have been given to us by supernatural inspiration when it has not, it is a fraud and ought to be exposed and rejected.

There is no false sect or heretical cult that does not have to depend upon additions to the Word of God. For instance, those who follow the teachings of Mormonism must add to the Bible that which was revealed to Joseph Smith on the golden plates that he dug up in the hills of New York State. The Bible plus! Those who follow Christian Science accept the Bible but would add to it what purported to be revelation from God received by Mary Baker Patterson Glover Eddy.

Seventh Day Adventism accepts not only the Bible but also the revelations that were received and were passed on by Ellen G. White. Those who follow Theosophy must add to the Bible the revelation that was given to Helena Petrovna. Jehovah's Witnesses supplement the Scripture with the writings of Charles Taze Russell and J. F. Rutherford. Need we go on?

The false cults begin with the Word of God, then relegate it to a place of secondary importance, while the writings of men are made the basis of understanding and interpretation of that which is contained in the Book of books. So we are faced with the questions, "What is the ministry of the Holy Spirit in inspiration? Is this Book which we hold in our hands the Bible, the Word of God in truth? Or do we need added revelations? Do we need the works of men to open up the teachings of Scripture to us? What is the work of the Spirit in inspiration?"

Peter has affirmed that the Spirit of God has revealed truth to men. This revelation might come to men in many different forms, but the channel of revelation was of secondary importance. The fact that the Holy Spirit revealed truth of necessity made that which He revealed to be truth. It could be no error.

Inspiration does not have to do with the revealing of truth, of making truth known to the minds of men. The doctrine of inspiration has to do with the recording of truth that was revealed by the Holy Spirit to men. What good would it do for God to reveal truth to men whose minds were too small to receive it, and too ignorant to understand it, and too childish to retain it, if provision were not made for revelation to be preserved, so that those who were not personally present to hear the revelation might know the revelation of God? And as we examine the Scriptures, we see that the Scripture purports to be not only a revelation from God by the Holy Spirit, but in addition, the Word of God, or the Bible, is the very truth of revelation preserved for us accurately by the inspiration of the Holy Spirit.

The Word of God is rationally defensible, and observations can be made that any intelligent man would have to accept. Yet we do not want to infer that the Bible depends upon the rational arguments of men for its support. However, there are certain rational presuppositions. If God is an intelligent Person and has a message, He will deliver it. That is inherent in the very nature of God. An infinite God must make Himself known, must reveal Himself. A second corollary to this is: Since God is an intelligent God, and does have a message and He has given it, that message will be accurately given. God would be involved in a lie if He were truth and yet revealed truth in such a way that the minds of men were deceived in the revelation that He gave. It must be presumed that a God of integrity will reveal Himself in an intelligent manner and that the message will be accurately given. Further, it is also logical for us to presume that the message will be divinely preserved in its purity and that it will be indestructible. If God revealed Himself, and revealed Himself accurately, the very purpose of revelation would be defeated if that revelation were immediately obliterated or forgotten, so that the knowledge of the truth was lost. These are presuppositions that we assume as we come to our consideration of the teaching of the Word of God itself.

The Bible is susceptible to a good many external proofs of its authority, its integrity, its inspiration. We do not want to dwell on them, for they are weak, of themselves, and it is not what we think about the Bible which substantiates it, but what the Bible has to say about itself. But we might mention briefly the fact of the *unity* of the Scripture: It was written in sixty-six different books by more than forty authors, over a period of more than fifteen hundred years. It was written by men who came from different walks of life: some of them fishermen, some shepherds, some farmers, some herdsmen; some had sat at the feet of the greatest teachers of their day, and others had had, as far as we can discern, no formal schooling at all. And yet, throughout this Book there is a unity so that there is no contradiction between the earliest book and the latest book written. There is a homogeneity about the whole that shows that behind the authors there was Someone who was guiding, controlling, keeping these men—in spite of their different backgrounds, languages, social cultures—from any error or contradiction in what they wrote. This very unity of the Book attests its inspiration by the Holy Spirit.

We should also consider the fact of its *historicity*. If you go into the realm of archaeology, which digs up what men have left behind, you will learn that no discovery has ever contradicted a single word written in the Word of God. If you delve into history you will find the same thing—no fact has ever been discovered that has disproved anything revealed in the Word of God. This cannot be said of any other volume that has ever been written.

The *extent* of the Bible's revelation is not of human origin because it reveals things that go far beyond the scope of the human mind. It reveals to us the facts about God which no man could ever know; it reveals to us the facts about heaven and about hell; it reveals not only the past, as history, but it accurately foretells the future. God has spoken in specific details concerning people, nations and events that would take place in years ahead and no man has ever found a prophecy of the Word of God which was not fulfilled exactly as it was spoken by the prophets. Some mathematician has figured that if you took the prophecies concerning the first coming of Christ, there is one chance in eighty-seven—with ninety-three zeros stretched out after it—that the prophecies in the Bible could be right by guess alone. The extent of the revelation authenticates that this Book is God-given. Its subject matter deals not with what is readily discernible to men, but it deals with what is unknown. It leads men out of their own ignorance into the realm of eternal truth, and only that which has come from God could lead men into the truth of God, unless men are able to understand and know and fathom the depths of the knowledge of God by their own intellect.

The Bible's presentation is *unprejudiced*. If we were writing a book, we certainly would leave out all the sins, iniquities, transgressions and failures of those about whom we were writing. But you pick up the Word of God and you find a perfectly open and frank presentation of the great heroes of faith. If this Book were written to glorify man, certainly the record of the fall of man would have been eliminated. There would have been no mention of the other great transgressions that we find so frequently in the Word of God. The very fact that it records the true nature of man, his sins and his need, evidences that it is a divine revelation.

Even the greatest writers recognize that, in the realm of *literature*, the Word of God is unsurpassed. We could point again to the fact of the *Christ-centeredness* of this Book, for the whole Word of God, from Genesis to Revelation, was designed to reveal a Person. All the Old Testament points to Him. The Gospels in the New Testament present Him to us. All the Epistles look back to Him and He is the Center of all. Certainly it is not a Book of human origin that can point everywhere to the Lord Jesus Christ.

Yet it is not these external evidences upon which we base
our belief in the Word of God. In the final analysis, the doctrine of inspiration is believed, not because its defenders are
able to give logical reasons why we ought to believe it, not
because the doctrine is logically defensible from these external considerations, but we believe that the Bible is the
inspired Word of God because the Bible itself so attests to the
fact. There is evidence within the Word of God itself that
this is a Book of no human origin; that it has come to us by
the Holy Spirit in order that we might have an accurate
record of what has been revealed. Read the words of Christ
to the Pharisees: "What think ye of Christ? whose son is he?
They say unto him, the son of David. He saith unto them,
How then doth David in spirit call him Lord . . ." (Matthew
22:42-43). The phrase "in spirit" shows us the origination
of David's statement concerning the Person of Christ. In Mark
12:36 Jesus said, "David himself said by the Holy Ghost,
The Lord said to my Lord, Sit thou on my right hand, till I
make thine enemies thy footstool." Notice that the Lord
Jesus Christ quotes Psalm 110 and says that David spoke *by the
Holy Ghost*. It was given as the Holy Ghost spoke to David.
In John 16:12-15 Christ anticipated more Scriptures to come
and spoke concerning the Holy Spirit: "he will shew you
things to come." Our Lord not only looks back and says that
the Old Testament was given by the Holy Spirit, but He also
says there is more Scripture yet to be written and the Holy
Spirit will do the work of speaking, of revealing, and of causing to be recorded the things concerning Himself.

We find that the Apostles make the same affirmation. In
Acts 1:16, Peter quotes from the Psalms and says: "Men and
brethren, this scripture must needs have been fulfilled, which
the Holy Ghost by the mouth of David spake before concern-

ing Judas, which was guide to them that took Jesus." Note:
The Holy Spirit spoke by the mouth of David. In Acts 28:25
we read: "And when they agreed not among themselves, they
departed, after that Paul had spoken one word, Well spake
the Holy Ghost by Esaias [that is, Isaiah] the prophet unto
our fathers, Saying, Go unto this people, and say, Hearing ye
shall hear, and shall not understand; and seeing ye shall see,
and not perceive." The Apostle Paul quotes the Old Testament and he refers to it as having come to us because the Holy
Spirit revealed a truth to Isaiah, and then controlled the lips
of Isaiah so that he spoke a message that had been revealed
to him. Consequently the message delivered was exactly the
message that God, the Holy Spirit, wanted the nation Israel
to have.

In II Peter 3:15-16 we have a word from Peter who has
spoken previously concerning the inspiration of Scripture by
the Holy Spirit. He says, "And account that the longsuffering
of our Lord is salvation; even as our beloved brother Paul
also according to the wisdom given unto him hath written
unto you." Paul's wisdom was not wisdom that he got because
he had sat at the feet of the greatest teachers, or because he
had reasoned it out himself during his long experience in
walking with Christ. It was wisdom given unto him by the
Spirit. Peter continues: "As also in all his epistles, speaking
in them of these things; in which are some things hard to be
understood, which they that are unlearned and unstable wrest,
as they do also the other scriptures, unto their own destruction." Now what are the other Scriptures? They are the same
Scriptures Peter spoke of in Acts 1:16: the Old Testament.
The interesting fact here is that the Apostle Peter, who has
affirmed that the Holy Ghost gave the Old Testament Scriptures, here affirms that the writings of the Apostle Paul are

also Scriptures and that they were given to him by a wisdom
not his own. This is Peter's affirmation of the fulfillment of
John 16:15, that the Spirit will show you things to come. And
when Paul wrote, Peter recognized those writings as having
been written because the Holy Spirit, who gave the Old Testament Scriptures, gave the message through the Apostle Paul.

Another interesting Scripture is I Timothy 5:18, where
the Apostle says, "For the scripture saith, Thou shalt not
muzzle the ox that treadeth out the corn." And "The labourer
is worthy of his reward." The Scripture that he quotes first
in this passage comes to us from Deuteronomy 25:4 and Paul
claimed that the Book of Deuteronomy, the Old Testament
Book of Moses, was Scripture. But then, in the last part of
the verse, he quotes Luke 10:7, the New Testament, and he
puts the New Testament Gospel of Luke with the Book of
Moses and refers to both as Scriptures. Thus we find that the
New Testament calls the Old Testament Scripture that was
given by the Holy Ghost; Peter said the writings of Paul are
Scriptures that were given to him by a wisdom not his own;
and Paul said that the Gospels are a part of Scripture, a
revelation from God by the Holy Spirit, and are given to us
by inspiration.

One of the clearest affirmations concerning the inspiration
of the Scripture is II Timothy 3:16. The Apostle has presented a very dark picture of the apostasy and unbelief that
will arise in the last days. It is no wonder that false doctrine
can creep into so many churches because the people know
absolutely nothing of doctrine itself. "Oh," they say, "we
revere the Word of God; we respect the Bible." But if you
ask them what the Bible teaches, they have not the faintest
idea. And the Apostle says there will be those who, because
they know nothing of the Word of God and know nothing

of doctrine, will be perverted in their minds, in their wills and in their walk. Timothy is to continue, "in the things which thou hast learned and hast been assured of, knowing of whom thou hast learned them" (II Timothy 3:14). Timothy had sat at the feet of the Apostle Paul and had been instructed by him in the truths of the Word of God. Timothy's defense against these false teachers, who were already appearing, was the word that had been taught him by Paul. That teaching would garrison him about and protect him from these false teachers. Paul affirms that Timothy, from childhood, had known the Holy Scriptures. The only Scriptures that Timothy had as a child were the Old Testament Scriptures, yet they were the Word of God. They were able to do the work of God in one who believed in God and accepted the Scriptures as God's revelation. ". . . from a child thou hast known the holy scriptures, which are able to make thee wise unto salvation through faith which is in Christ Jesus" (v. 15). The Old Testament bore witness to Jesus Christ. One who did not have the New Testament, but who examined the Old Testament and compared Christ to that which was revealed in it, would see that Jesus Christ fulfilled all that God's Messiah, God's Son, would do, and he would be led through those Scriptures to faith in the Person of Jesus Christ.

Then Paul makes this glorious affirmation: "All scripture is given by inspiration of God . . ." (v. 16). You will recognize that there are some who want to water down this translation and say, "All scripture *that is* given by inspiration of God is profitable." It certainly is true that all Scripture that *is* given by inspiration of God *is* profitable, but that reading infers that there are Scriptures that are not given by inspiration of God. Now is that what Paul is saying? While it is an allowable translation, it is not the preferable one. Paul said, "All scripture is given by inspiration of God." What does he include in this "All scripture"? To begin with, it includes all the Scriptures that Timothy had known as a child, everything from Genesis to Malachi. Further, it would include all the Scriptures that Peter spoke about, all the writings of the Apostle Paul. It would include that Scripture that Paul referred to, the Gospels. Thus, this includes not only the Old Testament, but the New Testament also.

What is Paul teaching us when he says, "All scripture is given by inspiration of God," or "All Scripture is God-breathed"? We are up against a rather clumsy rendering in English, and I don't know how we are going to get around it, because of the paucity of the English language. If we had a word "spire," meaning "to breathe" or "to spirate," or "spiraation," meaning "to breathe" or "breath," we could understand this English reading, but we don't have a word like that. Our word *inspiration* means "to breathe *into*." That translation has led some people to a false concept of what Paul is teaching. There are those who believe that the Bible is no more a supernatural Book than any other book, and that it is a product of the human mind. They might be willing to concede the fact that it was written by godly men who possessed a knowledge of truth above that held by the average man, but it is still a natural Book. But, when one picks up this Book, even though it is of natural origin, and begins to read it, God the Spirit hovers over and breathes into it so that a man may be inspired because the Spirit has breathed something into a natural product. It is as though a man might stand and view a glorious sunset and when the sun slips over the hill he breathes a sigh, and says "What an inspiration!" Something has been breathed into him. Or he may stand before a work of art, a piece of sculpture or a painting, and he may feel strangely moved and say, "It is inspiring." Or he may listen to Bach or Beethoven and because it stirs him he says "It was an inspiration to hear that." That is the way we use the word, but that is not the way it is used by Paul, for the Apostle is not saying that all Scripture is a natural product, but that God breathes into it so that it speaks to us or it inspires us in turn. That is an entirely false concept; it is contrary to true doctrine. This Greek word has nothing to say of *in*spiring or *in*spiration; it speaks only of a spiring or spiration. What the Apostle says is that all Scripture is given by the spiration of God, or by the breathing of God. That's why we sometimes translate this as "God-breathed." The Bible is God-breathed, so that the Book itself is the spiration of God. It is not something breathed into, but something that has been breathed out.

I like the definition that Dr. Lewis Sperry Chafer has given of this doctrine of inspiration: "The true doctrine of inspiration contends that God so directed the human authors, that, without destroying their own individuality, their literary style, their personal feelings, His complete and connected thought toward man was recorded." Now when we say that the Scriptures were breathed out by God the Holy Spirit, we are not suggesting that the Holy Spirit dictated, and that the human authors were scribes or secretaries who listened with an ear and then wrote down, stenographically, what was said. If that were true there would be no difference between the writings of Moses and the writings of Paul. There would be no peculiarities in the writings of Luke and the writings of Peter. They would be the same. We would not be able to discern and distinguish the personalities of the men who wrote as they are reflected in the books themselves. What we do believe is that the Holy Spirit of God directed and supervised these men who were appointed to write the Scriptures so that every single word that was written was the very word the Spirit of God wanted written to be the means of communicating truth and recording the revelation that had been given.

There are many different theories about inspiration. Some hold to what they call naturalistic inspiration; that, in effect, there is no real inspiration here at all. These authors were gifted men in the same way Shakespeare was a gifted man, and because of the natural gift they had they wrote what was superlative—but it was written apart from any operation of the Spirit of God.

There are others who hold to what they call a partial view of inspiration. They say some parts of Scripture are inspired, but not all. For instance, they would omit inspiration from all the books of history; there was no need to inspire history. The poetic books possess some inspiration. The books of doctrine in the New Testament are inspired. This leads to a rationalistic approach to the Scripture and allows no authority in the Book itself. We cannot accept this partial inspiration theory.

There are some who say that the Word of God was not inspired in its words, but rather the concepts were given to men and they were free to express these concepts the best way that they could. If this be true, we again have a naturalistic Book. True, they say, the revelation of the concepts was supernatural, but the reduction of these concepts to writing was purely natural. This view holds that we need to minimize the words and try to grasp the broad concept. This also produces a rational and mystical approach to the Word.

We want to affirm our faith in the doctrine of the verbal and plenary inspiration of the Word of God. I do not call this a theory, for I do not like to refer to the verbal plenary *theory* of inspiration. This is a settled fact. When we say that the Bible is verbally inspired, we mean that every single word written in the original language by the authors was under the sovereign direction of the Holy Spirit of God, and that the very word that He wanted recorded was recorded so that we have an accurate and trustworthy Book to which we can come to know truth. The necessity of verbal inspiration can be illustrated very simply. A man might dictate a letter to his secretary and say, "We will now fill your order," and when he gets the letter back from the typist, one letter is changed so that it reads: "We will not fill your order." Would the boss be willing to have that letter go out because it was so near to what he had dictated, differing in only one letter? You see how that one letter totally destroys and changes the whole meaning. If the Spirit of God did not supervise the very words in which this Book was written, then we have no assurance that it is trustworthy.

When we say that the Bible is plenarily inspired we mean that the Bible, in its entirety, was inspired by and is the Word of God. We recognize that the books of history may not have the same practical value as the books of doctrine; nor does some of the Old Testament wisdom literature have the same value as the Gospels in portraying Jesus Christ—but one is as much a part of divine revelation and as accurately given to us by inspiration as the rest.

How can we believe this? In II Timothy 3:16 the Apostle tells us the value of the Word of God. But the Word of God is of no value for any of these things unless it is given to us by inspiration. It is profitable for teaching. That is what the word *doctrine* means here. If this word is not the very Word of God, there is no point in teaching it. It is profitable for reproof. It sits as a judge of the lives and hearts and minds of men, and reproves men as there is need. It is profitable for correction. It can take that which is bent or broken and out of shape and make it straight again, and only that which had been given by inspiration of God could accomplish it. It is profitable for instruction in righteousness. The Word of God reveals the truth of a Holy God with all His righteous demands, and we may be instructed in righteousness because this is given to us by inspiration of God.

In Hebrews 4 we are taught what the Word of God will do, which it would have no power to do unless it was actually given by the Spirit's inspiration. The Apostle writes, "the word of God is quick . . ." (v. 12), or "living." It is alive because it has come from a living God. It can produce life. The Apostle Peter tells us that we were "born again, not of corruptible seed, but of incorruptible, by the word of God, which liveth and abideth for ever" (I Peter 1:23). The Bible is the revelation of a living God and it can impart life because it is living. ". . . the Word of God is . . . powerful . . ." (v. 12); it is active; it energizes. The Spirit of God can take the Word of God and move upon a heart or life that is absolutely dead and devoid of Spiritual life. The Word can produce this effect for the Word of God is powerful and it energizes. ". . . the word of God is . . . sharper than any twoedged sword, piercing even to the dividing asunder of soul and spirit, and of the joints and marrow . . ." (v. 12). This shows us the depths of penetration to which the Word of God can go. It does not deal with surface things and superficialities, but it can penetrate to the depths of the soul and the heart of man and lay bare before the man what he is and show him that he is liable to divine judgment. Only that which has been given by divine inspiration of God could do that. God has given us a revelation. God the Holy Spirit has so superintended the authorship of the Bible that it is authoritative and trustworthy. The Word of God claims for itself to be a complete and final revelation. The Spirit, who is truth, has revealed to man all the truth within this Book that it is necessary for a man to know concerning the things of God. We need not the added purported revelations of Joseph Smith or Mary Baker Eddy or Ellen G. White or any others, for the Spirit of God has given us the Word of God, which is authoritative and trustworthy. Upon it a man may build for time and for eternity. That is why the Apostle said to Timothy, the young minister, that he had one great obligation, to "Preach the word . . ." (II Timothy 4:2). Why? Because it is God's revelation, given by inspiration, and contains that which can make a man wise unto salvation.

4

THE MINISTRY OF THE SPIRIT BEFORE PENTECOST

THERE ARE FEW, IF ANY, VERSES IN ALL OF THE OLD TESTAMENT revelation concerning the Person and work of the Holy Spirit that have so upset God's children as the portion of the prayer of the Psalmist, recorded in Psalm 51:11: "take not thy holy spirit from me." As we have seen David fall into sin and listened to his prayer of confession, we have felt a real kinship with him, for even though we have not all sinned alike, we alike have all sinned since we have come to know Jesus Christ as a personal Saviour. Because we, like David, have fallen into sin, and have had to turn to God in confession, we have felt that we must pray as David prayed, "take not thy holy spirit from me." And much that is erroneous concerning the Person and work of the Holy Spirit has arisen from this passage of Scripture, for many teach that somehow we are in danger of committing some sin that will drive the Spirit from us, or that we can commit some unpardonable sin that will so grieve the Holy Spirit that He will be grieved away. In order that we might understand something of the teaching of the Word of God about the relationship of the Holy Spirit to the child of God, we want to go into the Old Testament to lay a foundation and to have you consider the subject of the Holy Spirit before the day of Pentecost and the ministry of the Holy Spirit in the old testament era.

We would recognize from the first chapter of the Book of

Genesis that the Holy Spirit was active from the very time of creation. We read in Genesis 1:2: "And the earth was without form, and void; and darkness was upon the face of the deep. And the Spirit of God moved [literally, brooded or hovered] upon the face of the waters." In the formation of this earth as a habitable place for man, the Holy Spirit was an active agent in *creation*. Further, we find that the Holy Spirit was the active agent, before the time of Christ, in *revelation*. All the prophets spoke as truth was revealed to them by the Holy Spirit. The Holy Spirit was likewise the agent in *inspiration*, for those to whom revelation was made became instruments by whom that revelation was written.

Consider now not the general ministry of the Holy Spirit in the Old Testament, but rather the ministry of the Holy Spirit to those who were God's instruments, to those who were believers, who received a gift of the Holy Spirit. We notice, as we go through the pages of the Word of God, that there was such an experience as the indwelling of the Holy Spirit in the Old Testament. The Lord Jesus, in revealing truth concerning the Holy Spirit in the upper room, divided the Holy Spirit's ministry into two parts: that before the day of Pentecost and that following the day of Pentecost. Christ said, "he dwelleth with you, and shall be in you" (John 14:17). "Dwelleth *with* you" is a reference to the relationship of the Holy Spirit to men before He came to take up His residence within all believers on the day of Pentecost. The phrase "and shall be *in* you" is the post-Pentecost experience, for on the day of Pentecost the Holy Spirit came to indwell every believer in the Lord Jesus Christ. In this present study we are considering our Lord's words when He said, "he dwelleth with you. . . ." In a later study we will be considering more of the second part of His words, "he . . . shall be in you."

We recognize that the Spirit of God possesses all of the

attributes of God the Father and God the Son. Since God the Father and God the Son are omniscient, that is, all-wise, the Spirit is no less omniscient. Since God the Father and God the Son are omnipresent, that is, everywhere present, the Holy Spirit was no less present in the Old Testament than the Father and the Son. When our Lord, in John 14:17, said, "he dwelleth with you," He was not referring only to the omnipresence of the Holy Spirit; that is, that the Holy Spirit is everywhere present and fills up this world and this universe with Himself. Jesus was speaking of a special relationship which was enjoyed by a chosen few, and the disciples were among those chosen ones who had been brought into a special relationship with the Holy Spirit so that it could be said, "he dwelleth with you." And that which was enjoyed by the disciples was enjoyed by selected individuals throughout the Old Testament.

A number of passages of Scripture may be cited to show that there were men who were indwelt by the Holy Spirit of God and who had this special privilege given to them by God. The first reference we find to this indwelling of the Holy Spirit is in Genesis 41:38, where we have a word from an idolatrous and heathen king. Pharaoh of Egypt spoke concerning one of God's chosen ones, Joseph: "Can we find such a one as this is, a man in whom the Spirit of God is?" I do not believe that Pharaoh understood what he was saying, for he was ignorant of the Trinity, ignorant of the third Person and ignorant of the Holy Spirit; but Pharoah recognized that there was something manifested in God's servant that was not observed in other men. It was something that Pharoah had never seen before, even though he had been surrounded by multitudes of priests in his own religion. This is a general reference, but it is an indication that the Spirit of God indwelt this man Joseph.

In Exodus 28 we find a reference to men who were given the gift of the Holy Spirit in order to enable them to work as skilled craftsmen in erecting and building the tabernacle in the wilderness. In Exodus 28:3 we read: "And thou shalt speak unto all that are wise hearted, whom I have filled with the spirit of wisdom, that they may make Aaron's garments to consecrate him, that he may minister unto me in the priest's office." And again, in Exodus 31:3-5, concerning the workmen who would erect the tabernacle, we read: "I have filled him with the spirit of God, in wisdom, and in understanding, and in knowledge, and in all manner of workmanship, To devise cunning works, to work in gold, and in silver, and in brass, And in cutting of stones, to set them, and in carving of timber, to work in all manner of workmanship." The tabernacle was to be erected according to a divine plan. There were to be no imperfections in its design, nor in the craftmanship with which it was built, and God gave the Holy Spirit as a gift to these craftsmen so that the work they accomplished with their hands should be a perfect work in order that there should be a temple in which God could dwell. God said, "I have filled him with the spirit of God. . . ."

In Numbers 11 we find that Moses associated with himself seventy men who were set apart to become counselors and advisers and assistants in the responsibility of supervising the nation Israel. God said, "I will come down and talk with thee there: and I will take of the spirit which is upon thee, and will put it upon them; and they shall bear the burden of the people with thee, that thou bear it not thyself alone" (v. 17). Now, as far as I can determine, the Scripture has not previously said that Moses was indwelt and empowered and made wise by the Spirit of God. Yet God said in this passage that He would take the Spirit that was given to Moses and would give it to these seventy. Thus we would deduce that, since the Spirit was taken from Moses and given to the seventy, Moses himself ministered by the gift of the Holy Spirit that was given to him. Notice in the same chapter that "the Lord came down in a cloud, and spake unto him, and took of the spirit that was upon him, and gave it unto the seventy elders . . ." (v. 25). God singled out not one man, as He had done with Joseph or Moses, but seventy men and gave them this gift. As far as we cen tell there were just these seventy men among all the multitudes of the children of Israel, besides Moses and perhaps Aaron, who possessed this particular gift of the Holy Spirit to empower them for this work of leadership.

From the Book of Judges we find that there were a number of men and women whom God raised up to be the successors of Moses and Aaron as administrators over the commonwealth of Israel. And of a number of these leaders it is said that God put the Spirit of God upon them. Gideon is representative of this group. In Judges 6:34 Scripture states, "the Spirit of the Lord came upon Gideon, and he blew a trumpet; and Abiezer was gathered after him." Then we have recorded the preparation of Gideon for the battle in which he and his three hundred men were victorious. But the significant thing is that Gideon ministered because "the Spirit of the Lord came upon Gideon. . . ." In reference to Samson, another one of the judges whom God raised up, Judges 13:25, says "the Spirit of the Lord began to move him at times in the camp of Dan between Zorah and Eshtaol." In Judges 14:6, it is recorded "the Spirit of the Lord came mightily upon him, and he rent him as he would have rent a kid, and he had nothing in his hand. . . ." Also, we read, "the Philistines shouted against him: and the Spirit of the Lord came mightily upon him, and the cords that were upon his

arms became as flax that was burnt with fire . . ." (Judges
15:14). Here was one raised up by God, upon whom the
Spirit of God came not once but repeatedly. And on a number of occasions, when there was need for a manifestation of
divine power, the Spirit of God specifically came upon Samson that he might do mighty feats by the power that was
given to him.

When we pass beyond the Judges, God began to raise up
kings to reign in Israel. The kings were given this gift of
the Holy Spirit. In reference to Saul, it is written: "it was
so, that when he had turned his back to go from Samuel, God
gave him another heart: and all those signs came to pass that
day. And when they came thither to the hill, behold, a company of prophets met him; and the Spirit of God came upon
him, and he prophesied among them" (I Samuel 10:9-10).
Saul, whom we characterize as a man of the flesh, was one
upon whom the Spirit of God came, and his mouth was
opened to declare God's message to the nation Israel. Concerning David we read: "Samuel took the horn of oil, and
anointed him in the midst of his brethren: and the Spirit of
the Lord came upon David from that day forward" (I Samuel
16:13).

We can't help but see the difference between Samson and
David. Of Samson it is said that the Spirit of the Lord came
repeatedly, at intervals, for different manifestations of the
Spirit's power. But of David it was said that the Spirit of the
Lord came upon him *from that day forward*. David had a
most unique experience in his relationship with the Spirit
of God in that the Spirit came upon him in a way He had
come upon no other individual in the Old Testament. At
least, of no other one is it stated that the Spirit of God came
upon him "from that day forward." As you read through the

Psalms you wonder how a man could write such exalted praise to God. The answer is found in I Samuel 16:13: The empowerment of the Spirit of God came upon David so that he could be called "the sweet singer of Israel." So often we find the interpretation given that David spent so much time alone out on the hillsides as a shepherd, and he had little to do but to muse; and while he was musing, he received an inspiration from nature, and out of the inspiration that came from nature he wrote these exalted Psalms. Scripture says the Spirit of the Lord came upon him, and by inspiration of the Holy Spirit he wrote.

When we pass beyond the time of the kings to the time of the prophets, Daniel was one recognized as being blessed with the presence of the Holy Spirit. Again the testimony comes from a godless king, for Nebuchadnezzar testifies that Daniel is one "in whom is the spirit of the holy gods . . ." (Daniel 4:8). Again, "I have even heard of thee, that the spirit of the gods is in thee, and that light and understanding and excellent wisdom is found in thee" (Daniel 5:14). This testimony comes from a man who does not know the true God. It comes from a polytheist. Yet this one who worshiped many gods recognized that this was not natural wisdom and understanding and light that dwelt in Daniel; he recognized it as supernatural. While Nebuchadnezzar did not understand anything about the Person and work of the Holy Spirit as we are privileged to know through the Word of God, he recognized and bore testimony that Daniel was one whose life was under the domination and control of the Spirit of God.

From these references you can see that men in the Old Testament did have the privilege of an experience with the Holy Spirit. He dwelt with them; He came upon them; He was said to dwell in them; He gave to them wisdom and understanding that were greater than would be found naturally within man.

Now we want to consider something of the features of this indwelling. There are some who feel that there is no difference whatsoever between the Old Testament relationship to the Holy Spirit and the New Testament relationship. The danger in failing to observe this distinction lies in the fact that we may be tempted to pattern our experience with the Holy Spirit by what was true in the Old Testament. If there is no difference, if what was true in the Old is also true in the New, we then must take the Old Testament relationship to the Spirit of God as our norm and standard. If men in the Old Testament could lose the Holy Spirit, men in the New Testament can lose the Holy Spirit. If men in the Old Testament could sin away the presence of the Holy Spirit, we may sin away His presence. But I want you to understand from our Lord's words that, in the day in which our Lord was living, He was anticipating something entirely new, so that what was to come would be entirely different from what existed when our Lord was upon the earth. In John 7:37, "In the last day, that great day of the feast, Jesus stood and cried, saying, If any man thirst, let him come unto me, and drink. He that believeth on me, as the scripture hath said, out of his belly shall flow rivers of living water." Notice our Lord's interpretation and explanation in verse 39: "But this spake he of the Spirit, which they that believe on him *should* [that's future, isn't it?] receive. . . ." It is not what they *have* received, but what they *should* receive in the future, "for the Holy Ghost was not yet given; because that Jesus was not yet glorified."

In what way did our Lord say the Holy Spirit is not

yet given when we have just seen a number of Scriptures that have shown us the Holy Spirit was given to some men? You see, our Lord is anticipating something entirely new which is to come, and what was true in the Old Testament was in no sense the pattern or the norm for what would be true when the Holy Spirit would be given. The Holy Spirit was not yet given in the sense in which He would be given on the day of Pentecost, nor was the relationship that then existed what would exist when the Holy Spirit had come in His fullness.

When you come once more to the upper room discourse in John 14-16, the disciples are trying to prevent our Lord from going away. Peter frequently fell into that trap; he tried to prevent the Lord Jesus Christ from going to Jerusalem because the Lord had said that His procession to Jerusalem was a procession to death and ultimate separation from them. When they came together in the upper room our Lord began to talk about His death. The disciples asked a very plain question: "Why is it necessary for you to go? Why can't you stay with us, for we are perfectly satisfied with the relationship which we have?" And Christ had to tell them that if He does not go away the Spirit cannot come, for the Spirit cannot and will not come until the Son goes to the Father. He said to them, "And I will pray the Father, and he shall give you another Comforter, that he may abide with you for ever; Even the Spirit of truth . . ." (John 14:16-17); "But the Comforter, which is the Holy Ghost, whom the Father will send in my name, he shall teach you all things, and bring all things to your remembrance, whatsoever I have said unto you" (v. 26); "Ye have heard how I said unto you, I go away, and come again unto you. If ye loved me, ye would rejoice, because I said, I go unto the Father: for my

Father is greater than I" (v. 28). Our Lord, as He answers the question, "Lord, why must you go away?" replies, "I must go away because there is to be something entirely new in the ministry of the Holy Spirit, and if I don't go away He can't come, and if He can't come, you'll never enter into the fullness of the blessing that God has for you." What Jesus reveals is the fact that the features of the Spirit's ministry in the Old Testament are quite different from the features that would exist after the Lord Jesus Christ goes to the Father and the Father sends the Spirit to this earth to dwell within believers.

There are three essential features of the Spirit's indwelling in the Old Testament. In the first place, the indwelling was not universal; it was not for everyone who was rightly related to God. A few of the Old Testament saints had this experience, but only a few. There were multitudes upon multitudes who knew God in a personal relationship, whose sins had been forgiven, who never had one day of consciously being under the control of the Spirit of God, assured of the indwelling presence and the empowerment of the Spirit of God because the Spirit had come upon them and dwelt within them. If you do not recognize this fact, you are going to be led into the error that there is a second work of grace for men today, and until and unless you have had that second work of grace you will never have the Holy Spirit dwelling within you. And there are many who are begging and pleading and praying for a second work of grace because, since there were only a few in the Old Testament upon whom the Spirit came, it must be true that He only comes on a few today. They say, "I want to be like Moses, or Joseph, or Samson, or David, upon whom the Spirit came." Consequently they are begging and seeking and pleading that God will give them something when, praise God! that gift has already been given the very moment you accept Jesus Christ as personal Saviour.

The Holy Spirit in the Old Testament was not universal. He came upon a very few selected individuals; He came upon them to give them special privileges—to empower their hands with skill, or to open up their tongues to speak—or to give them ability to lead or guide the nation Israel, but it was a sovereign act of God. Neither Moses nor Joseph, nor Gideon, nor Samson was indwelt because of some special thing within the man. They did not do something to get the Holy Spirit's presence. God gave them that gift sovereignly. They had nothing to do with it nor could they get it by asking for it. God chose them and made them His instruments. The first important distinction to observe, then, is that the Holy Spirit's indwelling in the Old Testament was not universal for all believers.

The second thing that we would observe, and we have already touched on this, is that the Holy Spirit came upon men to empower them to some special service. With Moses and the seventy, it was to lead; with Daniel, it was to prophesy; with the artisans, it was to construct a tabernacle which should be a habitation of God. The ministry of the Holy Spirit was not just to produce fellowship, not to bring those who were indwelt into some intimacy of relationship with God the Father, or the Son, or the Spirit Himself. It was not for acts of worship, or praise, or the intimacy of abiding in Christ—but it was given to perform some special work. The purpose of the indwelling in the New Testament far exceeds that of the Old. While there is empowerment to work today, this is but one of His purposes.

A third thing we notice in the Old Testament is that the

indwelling was temporary. Several passages of Scripture reveal this fact. Samson was indwelt by the Spirit of God, but later Delilah said, "The Philistines be upon thee, Samson. And he awoke out of his sleep, and said, I will go out as at other times before, and shake myself. *And he wist not that the Lord was departed from him*" (Judges 16:20). Now what does it mean, "the Lord was departed from him"? We were told again and again that it was the Spirit of the Lord that was the power of Samson. When the Spirit left, Samson's power was gone. But he knew not that the Holy Spirit, who had come to indwell him, had now departed from him so he was bereft of the Spirit's empowerment. The Holy Spirit's ministry to Samson was temporary.

We have seen previously that Saul was empowered by the Holy Spirit when the Spirit came upon him. But we read, "But the Spirit of the Lord departed from Saul, and an evil spirit from the Lord troubled him" (I Samuel 16:14). Here was one who had wrought mighty deeds by the power of the Spirit, but now, because of the temporary nature of the Spirit's indwelling, the Spirit has departed and Saul is bereft of the presence and power of the Holy Spirit within him.

In Psalm 51 we find David praying because of the enormity of his public sin, a sin that could not be hidden from the nation over which he ruled. Here was a man with whom the Spirit had come to abide, but David knew full well that his relationship to the Holy Spirit was not guaranteed to be a permanent thing, and that because of his transgressions the Spirit might leave him and cast him aside as God had cast aside Samson and Saul. God might take another instrument to be the one through whom He worked. And so David asked God, on the basis of His mercy, to purge him from his sin; to apply the blood of sacrifice and the water of cleansing.

Then he prays, "take not thy holy spirit from me" (v. 11). David was praying a prayer that was perfectly legitimate in his day, but he was praying a prayer that no child of God has any business to pray today.

You ask, "Why not?" The reply is in two contrasts between the Old Testament and the New Testament relationship to the Holy Spirit. There are many things we will have to say about the Holy Spirit's ministry in the New Testament in our future studies; for the present, notice these two points. First, the Old Testament indwelling was not universal; it was for a few. In the New Testament, it is universal and every one who has accepted Jesus Christ as his personal Saviour has received the gift of the indwelling presence of the Spirit of God. A good passage to look at would be that familiar one in Romans 8:9: "But ye are not in the flesh, but in the Spirit, if so be that the Spirit of God dwells in you. Now if any man have not the Spirit of Christ, he is none of his." Observe very carefully that the presence of the Spirit and the possession of eternal life are coequal and coexistent in the experience of the believer. The Apostle does not leave any room for the teaching that a man may be born again and then at some subsequent time, in response to prayer, or surrender, or contrition, or petition, receive the Spirit as an added gift or a second blessing. The Apostle says that if a man does not have the Spirit of Christ, he is *none* of His. Paul teaches the same truth in I Corinthians 6:19. The Apostle is writing to just about the sorriest lot of Christians that you can find anywhere in the New Testament. (If a preacher is having trouble with his congregation, but hesitates to mention their sins, the best thing for him to do is to start through I Corinthians. By the time he gets through II Corinthians he will have hit about every sin that can possibly creep into an assembly of believers.) Paul is writing to a group that has moral problems, doctrinal problems, schisms and heresies. And yet, notice what Paul says about them: "What? know ye not [as sorry a lot as you are] that your body is the temple of the Holy Ghost which is in you, which ye have of God, and ye are not your own?" Paul isn't saying, "I'm writing to you, who used to be a group of sinners, but you've gotten the second blessing and you have been sanctified, and now, because of what you are, you have the Holy Spirit." No. The basis of his plea is the fact that they have received the gift of salvation and the gift of the Holy Spirit, which is their *universal* experience.

The second great contrast is in the duration of the indwelling. Hear the words of our Lord: "that he might abide with you for ever" (John 14:16). Christ has promised that out of the believer's innermost being shall flow rivers of living water, and that the Spirit, who is given to every child of God universally, is given permanently. That is why after some sin you need not pray, "Father, don't take your Spirit from me." You are insulting God; you are calling God a liar when you speak that prayer today, for God said that His gift to us is a permanent gift, and it is for every child of God.

There is one more thing that we want to mention concerning the work of the Holy Spirit in the Old Testament. We are in danger of losing this fact because what we refer to is recorded in the New Testament. Historically the New Testament does not begin with the Book of Matthew; it begins with the Book of Acts, because all that is recorded in the four Gospels took place before the death of Christ. Of course, the Gospels do record His resurrection but our Lord was living under the Old Testament ministry and economy of the Holy Spirit, when the Holy Spirit came upon a few select individuals to empower them to some work, and He did not come permanently. The one fact that we perhaps would overlook is given to us in the third chapter of John's Gospel—that the Holy Spirit in the Old Testament was, as He is today, the agent in the new birth.

You ask me, "Do you believe men were born again before the day of Pentecost?" Of course, I do! No man ever came into the family of God apart from being born into that family. No man ever came into the family of God apart from the work of the Holy Spirit. That was why, when the Lord Jesus sat down with one of the leaders of Israel, He said to Nicodemus, "Except a man be born of water and of the Spirit, he cannot enter into the kingdom of God. That which is born of the flesh is flesh; and that which is born of the Spirit is spirit" (John 3:5-6). Speaking nearly three years before His death, Christ said that the Spirit's work in the Old Testament was to bring men to a new birth, to a regeneration. That is one aspect of the Spirit's ministry that did not change after Pentecost. The Spirit of God is the agent who gave new birth to every one who came into the family of God. On the authority of the Word of God, we affirm that the Holy Spirit is doing this work today. As one receives Jesus Christ as his personal Saviour, by the Spirit of God he is born into the family of God. Any man in the Old Testament who was rightly related to God, was rightly related because of the Spirit's work. The great change is not in what the Spirit did for a man. The great change between the Old Testament and the New Testament is in the changed relationship to the Spirit of the one for whom the Spirit had affected the new birth.

How we can praise God, we who have come to know Jesus Christ as personal Saviour, that the indwelling is universal for every child of God! It is permanent and we need not pray, "Take not thy Spirit from us," for God has promised He will never lease us, nor fail us, nor forsake us. Nor need we pray, "Send the Spirit to dwell with me," for the Spirit has come and has taken up residence within us.

5

THE MINISTRY OF THE SPIRIT TO THE WORLD

BECAUSE BELIEVERS ARE PRIMARILY CONCERNED WITH THE ministries of the Holy Spirit following His advent into the body which is His temple on the day of Pentecost, we somehow have come to feel that the Holy Spirit was inactive before that great event recorded in Acts 2. We focus our attention upon the great ministries of the Spirit to the child of God, such as the regenerating work of the Spirit, the baptizing work, the indwelling work, the filling work, the sealing work—all ministries which began on the day of Pentecost and continue throughout this age. It is not surprising that we should dwell upon these ministries of the Spirit, for they are the ministries in which we, as believers, are the most vitally concerned. And yet, the Word of God reveals the fact that the Holy Spirit had a ministry that began at the time of creation, and which has continued unchanged down through the ages. This is His ministry to the world in general.

In the Garden of Eden a perfect society existed. Man was not a lawless being when he was created by God and placed in the Garden of Eden in a perfect environment. He was not created a rebel; he was created in subjection to the Creator. That perfect society existed for some time—how long we do not know. But the tempter came into the Garden of Eden and, by solicitation, brought Eve from the place of subjection to the place of disobedience. Adam quickly followed in her disobedience. Lawlessness was introduced into what had been a lawful state and place. The nature of Adam, by the fall, was completely changed. Instead of being a friend of God, he was at enmity with God. Instead of enjoying companionship with God, he was separated from God by a great gulf. The visible sign of that separation was the expulsion of Adam and Eve from the Garden. Instead of being in subjection to the Word of God and the commandment of God, Adam and Eve and their descendants were in rebellion against God. Instead of producing the fruits of their untried innocence, with which they were endowed from creation, there flowed from Adam and his descendants the multitude of sins that Paul refers to as "the lust of the flesh" (Galatians 5:17). A very graphic picture is given by Paul: "Now the works of the flesh are manifest, which are these; Adultery, fornication, uncleanness, lasciviousness, Idolatry, witchcraft, hatred, variance, emulations, wrath, strife, seditions, heresies, envyings, murders, drunkenness, revellings, and such like . . ." (vv. 19-20). There were sins in the moral realm, in the religious realm, in the social realm; there were sins that manifested themselves externally; there were sins that raged within the sinner himself. Such was the picture of the society that had been brought into existence by the rebellion of man.

Yet, as we look upon the world, whether back in Adam's day or in our own day, we see that there are men who live good lives. They are morally upright and respectable. They are not wallowing in the depths of iniquity. They are fine, upstanding citizens, men of moral integrity, respected and trusted, even though some of them are without a knowledge of our Lord Jesus Christ. How is it that men in whose hearts are the seeds of corruption, within whose breasts dwell the sin nature which is a rebel against God, can live in obedience and subjection to law and can manifest goodnesses as the world evaluates goodnesses? How do you explain a law-abiding citizen in the midst of lawlessness? That brings us to the first great work of the Holy Spirit in reference to the world at large. The Holy Spirit is a restrainer of sin, and it is His ministry to curb the lawlessness of the human heart, to keep the rebellion against God from getting out of hand. As evil as man is and as lawless as society is, man is not as bad as he could be, and society has not degenerated to the depths to which it could descend. This ministry of the Holy Spirit that began at the time of the fall in the Garden of Eden, and has continued to the present day, is a deterrent to lawlessness in the world.

Society had progressed, developed and expanded, but it had not become more righteous. Rather, it had become more degenerate. Men descended into sin to the point that God said, "My Spirit shall not always strive with man . . ." (Genesis 6:3). This is an announcement that a judgment by flood is about to descend upon the earth. The reason that the flood had not come earlier was because the Spirit of God had done a restraining work; He had set bounds as to the depths to which men could descend and beyond which they could not go. But when men refused to heed the restraining work of the Spirit of God and desired to go beyond the bounds which He had set, God said that He would bring a flood judgment which would wipe out the rebels from the face of the earth.

The prophet Isaiah gives us another glimpse of this ministry of the Spirit. The prophet looked forward to the time when the nation Israel would be redeemed and would be brought into subjection to her Messiah, when the Messiah would reign in righteousness upon the earth: "So shall they fear the name of the Lord from the west, and his glory from the rising of the sun. When the enemy shall come in like a flood, the Spirit of the Lord shall lift up a standard against him" (Isaiah 59:19). The Holy Spirit is the one who prevented evil from spreading, from sending out its tentacles to envelop the nation Israel. And it is the Spirit of God who will set restraining bounds beyond which lawlessness, or evil, cannot go. When evil shall come in like a flood, the Spirit of God shall lift up a standard against it.

Paul gives us the most extended treatment on this ministry. The Apostle wrote to the Thessalonians concerning a very practical problem that faced them. There were some who were undergoing intense persecutions. They had been told by Paul that before the Lord Jesus Christ comes back to this earth to reign there would be a time of tribulation upon the earth. Paul had also told them, in I Thessalonians 4, that before tribulation came upon the earth, believers would be translated into the presence of the Lord so that they would not see that tribulation. But some who were going through tribulation were perplexed with a theological problem: Could it be that we have missed the translation, or the rapture, of the church? Could these tribulations which we are experiencing be the tribulations which precede the second coming of Christ? And Paul told them that even though they are going through persecutions, there is sufficient reason for them to know that they are not in the persecutions and judgments of the tribulation period.

The first great reason that the Apostle states is that the departure, or the falling away, has not yet come. He says in a letter, "Let no man receive you by any means: for that day [that is, the Day of the Lord, the judgments of the tribulation period] shall not come, except there come a falling away [or a departure] first . . ." (II Thessalonians 2:3). Now, whether the departure be the departure of the saints to meet the Lord, or whether it be the departure of the church from the true doctrine, is beside the point here. According to either view Paul is giving a reason to prove they cannot yet be in the tribulation period.

The second proof is stated at the end of verse 3: "that day shall not come, except . . . that man of sin be revealed, the son of perdition." The tribulation will begin when the head of the federated states of Europe makes a covenant with the nation Israel, to guarantee them their rights in the land of Palestine. This one is called "the beast" in Revelation 13; he is called here "the man of sin, or the lawless one." He is called the "son of perdition" because he is energized by Satan. Paul says that they can know that they cannot yet be in the tribulation period because this man of sin, this lawless one, has not yet appeared on the world scene to make his covenant with the nation Israel.

Paul then proceeds to tell them that even though Satan is trying to put his world-ruler on the throne of world government, there is Someone who is preventing Satan's purpose from being realized: "ye know what withholdeth . . ." (v. 6). That word, translated "withhold," is the Greek word which means "to restrain." Read it that way and you will get the point of what Paul is saying: "You know what restrains that he, the man of sin, might be revealed in his own time. For the mystery of lawlessness does already work." That is, Satan is trying to put his world dictator onto the throne of world government, but he has not succeeded in doing it. He has had his hand-picked men in every generation, so that if the door were opened for his plan to emerge, he would be ready to move into operation. But, Paul says, you know what restrains, so that Satan cannot put his man on the throne. He adds, "the mystery of iniquity doth already work: only he who now letteth [hinders], will let [keep on hindering], until he be taken out of the way. And then shall that Wicked [one] be revealed" (v. 7).

What the Apostle is teaching here is the same thing that John teaches us when he says, "this is that spirit of antichrist, whereof ye have heard that it should come; and even now already is it in the world" (I John 4:3). Paul and John tell us that Satan has a program, and he is not waiting until the end of the age to try to put it into operation. Satan was trying, at the very time that John and Paul lived, to promote his program. But all the time he was working to bring world government under his control and put the lawless one on the throne of government, there was Someone restraining and withholding, or preventing Satan from putting his master-piece in a place of world power. The restrainer of II Thessalonians 2 is the same one referred to in Genesis 6:3 and Isaiah 59:19. The restrainer is the Holy Spirit, who says to Satan or to any lawless movement, "You can go so far and no further."

We might ask the question, "How does the Holy Spirit do His work of restraining? Does He do it sovereignly, or does He work through some means?" We, of course, would not question for a moment that the Spirit, as the omnipotent One, can by His own power put limits beyond which a lawless one cannot go. But from the Word of God we discover that there are several instruments which the Spirit uses in His ministry as a restrainer. For instance, we find that the Holy Spirit works through human government. Paul says, "Let every soul be subject unto the higher powers. For there is no power but of God: the powers that be are ordained of God" (Romans 13:1). He is speaking of governmental powers in that verse. Notice that he says, these powers are ordained of God. "Whosoever therefore resisteth the power [that is, the governor, or the king, or the president], resisteth the ordinance of God. . . . rulers are not a terror to good works, but to the evil. Wilt thou then not be afraid of the power? do that which is good, and thou shalt have praise of the same: For he [that is, the governor] *is the minister of God to thee for good*. But if thou do that which is evil, be afraid; for he beareth not the sword in vain: for he is a minister of God, a revenger to execute wrath upon him that doeth evil" (vv. 2-4). Here we find that God has given human government the power to put bounds upon lawlessness and to curb unrighteousness. God has subjected men to the authority of government, so that government is one of the agencies that the Spirit of God uses in lifting up a standard against evil. We frequently get emotionally involved in the question as to whether capital punishment is right. The Word of God says that human government has the power of death in order to curb lawlessness and to punish the evildoer. And it is this right given to government which is a deterrent to lawlessness. What is one of the best ways to make you check your speedometer when you are driving down the road? See a man on a motorcycle ahead or notice a police car in the rear mirror! The very presence of one who has authority to enforce obedience to the law is a deterrent to lawlessness. This is one of the instruments the Spirit uses.

The revelation of judgment of evildoers before a righteous and holy God is another deterrent to lawlessness. I am not speaking about believers in this connection, but about unbelievers. There is planted in the heart of unbelievers the sense of responsibility to God. An unbeliever is faced with the expectation of being judged by a holy and righteous God. It is the Holy Spirit who brings to men the consciousness of coming judgment. In Hebrews 9:27 it is written: "it is appointed unto men once to die, but after this the judgment." You don't have to be taught from the Word of God that, following death, there must be a divine reckoning. That consciousness is written across the mind and the heart of even godless men by the work of the Holy Spirit. It is that fear of judgment that is an instrument used by the Spirit to curb lawlessness, or to restrain men. Again, in Hebrews, the writer says there is "a certain fearful looking for of judgment and fiery indignation, which shall devour the adversaries" (10:27). Dread and terror grips a man because of the consciousness of judgment to come. Peter speaks of mockers who had arisen, who were scoffing at the fact of a coming judgment. Even in their unbelief they were conscious of coming judgment, but because God had been patient and had not judged them, they felt that God would entirely pass over judgment. Peter had to remind them that "the heavens and the earth, which are now, by the same word are kept in store, reserved unto fire against the day of judgment and perdition of ungodly men" (II Peter 3:7). But, "The Lord is not slack concerning his promise . . ." (v. 9). Judgment will fall! Even though scoffers may minimize the idea of approaching judgment because of the patience of God, yet that consciousness of judgment is ingrained in every man's heart and mind. So it is scarcely ever necessary to prove to an unsaved man that he will be judged for his sins. That is an accepted fact. The unsaved man knows it, and he is terrified at the thought of it. Where did he get it? It is the ministry of the Holy Spirit who would use the expectation of judgment to restrain men in sin, because of the fear of judgment to come.

There is a third way by which the Spirit works to restrain,

and it is related to the second. He works through conscience. Paul writes that the Gentiles "shew the work of the law written in their hearts, their conscience also bearing witness, and their thoughts the mean while accusing or else excusing one another" (Romans 2:15). The subject of conscience is very wide, and it is impossible for us to cover it in any detail. But we would mention one fact: No people, no matter how degraded, no matter how spiritually blind, no matter how steeped in paganism, or idolatry, have ever been discovered who do not have a conscience that bears witness to the difference between right and wrong. The only ones in whom conscience is not found are those who are deprived of mental faculties. Conscience exists in men, universally. There is that law of conscience within them that, even though it may be dulled or stifled or ignored, even though it may be untrustworthy because of the degeneracy of man, yet it is lifting its voice, accusing or else excusing any course of conduct.

No one has ever been able to define conscience. Philosophers and psychologists try unsuccessfully to define it in terms of one's culture or mores. We suggest conscience is the voice of the Holy Spirit, the omnipresent One who restrains, reproves, rebukes and convicts men of their sin. Conscience is the universal witness of the Holy Spirit in the discharge of His ministry as a restrainer.

A fourth channel that the Spirit may use is suggested to us in John's Gospel. Our Lord says that the believers are going to be hated by the world (15:18). Why are they going to be hated? Because they belong to Christ and the world hated Christ. Why did the world hate Christ? He tells us, "If I had not come and spoken unto them, they had not had sin: but now they have no cloke [that is, no pretext or covering] for their sin" (15:22). And then He says, "when the Comforter is come, whom I will send unto you from the Father, even the Spirit of truth, which proceedeth from the Father, he shall testify of me; And ye also shall bear witness . . ." (15:26-27). What is our Lord talking about in this context? He is talking about the fact of sin. And the life that the believer lives before the world will be that which will convict the world and restrain the world in sin. The authority given to government, the revelation of coming judgment, the voice of the Spirit which is conscience, and the life the believer lives before the world—all may be used by the Spirit of God to restrain the world in its iniquity.

We are a blessed people because we live in a land where the restraining work of the Spirit is more manifest than in a great many other areas of the earth. Who would want to change places, for instance, with one in the heart of Africa or the jungles of South America? What is the difference? The difference is in the restraining work of the Holy Spirit. We ought to get down and thank God that we are privileged to live where the Spirit's ministry is manifested.

There is a second work of the Spirit to the world, the work in reproving. If you will, change the word "reprove" to the word "convict." The concept of the word "reprove" has changed because it suggests mild correction, and Christ is talking about the convicting work of the Spirit (John 16). Our Lord promised that when He went to the Father He would send the Holy Spirit, and when the Holy Spirit would come, "he will reprove [convict] the world . . ." (v. 8). He will convict the world of sin, of righteousness, and of judgment.

This passage has been so frequently misunderstood. We read it as though Christ said, "He will reprove the world of sin, and of righteousness, and of judgment"—of sin, namely the sin of unbelief: "they believe not on me"; of righteousness: namely, that "I go to my Father"; of judgment: the judgment of "the prince of this world" (vv. 9-11). We take the last part of each verse as though it were explanatory of the first part. Though this is true, it is not the truth that our Lord is giving here.

There are three great areas in which the Spirit will convict: He will convict of sin *because;* He will convict of righteousness *because;* He will convict of judgment *because.* The three "because" phrases tell us why the Holy Spirit has to do His work of convicting. He will convict of sin because "they believe not on me." If they did believe, He would not have to do His work of convicting of sin. Why not? Because, the very moment one accepts Jesus Christ as personal Saviour, "There is therefore now no condemnation [judgment] to them which are in Christ Jesus . . ." (Romans 8:1). We are washed, we are sanctified, we are justified by the blood of Christ Jesus. There is no basis of accusation whatsoever against one who has accepted Christ as his personal Saviour. John gives us the Word of our Lord that when the Spirit comes He will have to convict the world of sin because the world will not believe so that their sins can be removed.

The Spirit will convict the world of righteousness because; "I go to my Father, and ye see me no more." When Jesus Christ was in the world, He convicted the world of its sins. That is why we read in John 15:22: "If I had not come and spoken unto them, they had not had sin, but now they have no cloke for their sin." The Holy Spirit will continue the work of convicting men of the need for righteousness. And, further, He will convict the world that righteousness is available to any man because Jesus Christ is gone into the presence of the Father. When Christ died, He offered His blood as a sacrifice for sin. When He ascended, He ascended as a Priest to offer before God the benefits of His death. If God had not accepted the death of Christ as the payment for sin, He would have expelled that One who assayed to be a Priest. The fact that God did not expel the Son from heaven when He would begin a Priestly ministry is public sign that the sacrifice has been accepted, that righteousness is available to all men. The Spirit will convict of righteousness because the Son has gone to the Father. The world needs a Convicter because righteousness has been provided but is being rejected.

The Holy Spirit will convict the world of judgment, and the world *needs* to be convicted of judgment because the prince of this world is judged. Those who were born into this world were born into a relationship to the prince of this world. They are his subjects, members of his family. When the father is judged, the children are judged. When Satan is judged at the cross, all in Satan's kingdom are judged with him. And if Satan cannot be exempted from the effects of judgment, how can those who are under him expect to escape the consequences of judgment? So the Spirit has come into the world to do a work to the world. He will convict the world of sinfulness because men have not accepted the righteousness God has provided. He will convict the world of righteousness because righteousness has been rejected. He will convict the world of judgment because, when the prince of the world was judged, all his subjects were judged with him. When any man experiences the pangs of guilt for his sins, it is evidence that the Spirit is in the world to convict the world concerning the things of God.

There is a third area of the Spirit's work to the world. He not only restrains sin; He not only reproves sinners; but also He reveals that Jesus Christ is the Saviour. Our Lord was

speaking to believers in John 16:14 when He said, "He shall
glorify me: for he shall receive of mine, and shall shew it
unto you." But the truth is applicable to unbelievers as well.
Any man, who comes to know Jesus Christ as personal
Saviour, comes to know Him because the Spirit of God has
taken away the blindness from the sinner's eyes and the
deafness from the sinner's ears; He has let him see Jesus
Christ and hear God's offer of salvation. The Spirit of God
has energized that dead will so that man might reach out and
receive Jesus Christ as a personal Saviour.

In speaking to Nicodemus, our Lord said, "as Moses lifted
up the serpent in the wilderness, even so must the Son of
man be lifted up (John 3:14). He was likening Himself to the
serpent of brass that was put up on a pole. Christ also said,
"I, if I be lifted up from the earth, will draw all men unto
me" (John 12:32). That lifting up to which He referred was
the resurrection. Jesus Christ was saying, "I, if I be lifted up
out of the grave and received into glory, will draw all men
unto myself." How is He drawing men? It is by the Spirit
of God restraining, convicting and revealing Jesus Christ as
the Way, the Truth and the Life.

Our Lord stood at the graveside of Lazarus and did a very
strange thing. He began to speak to the corpse that had
already begun to decay. He spoke, and expected that corpse
to hear. He issued an authoritative command: "Lazarus,
come forth" (John 11:43), and Lazarus heard, responded and
emerged from the grave. Lazarus was given an ear to hear;
his body was given the power to respond, the ability to move,
even though bound hand and foot. The Spirit of God takes
one who, like Lazarus, was dead, bound by death, bound by
the grave clothes, and He reveals Jesus Christ; lets the dead,
sightless eyes look upon Him; lets the deaf ears hear Him

say, "Whosoever will may come"; lets that one respond to God's offer of salvation and take it as a free gift. When the Spirit reveals Jesus Christ, He does it in just one way, through the Word of God. That is why Peter says we were born again, "not of corruptible seed, but of incorruptible, by the word of God, which liveth and abideth for ever (I Peter 1:23). That is why, when Paul sent forth Timothy to preach, he told him to "Preach the word . . ." (II Timothy 4:2). Paul wrote, "faith cometh by hearing, and hearing by the word of God" (Romans 10:17). The Spirit of God will take the Word of God, use it as that agency by which He restrains, by which He reproves, but above all, by which He will reveal Jesus Christ as the One who can remove sin from the sinner; remove judgment from the one under death; who can give righteousness to the one who is unrighteous.

These are ministries which the Spirit of God undertook at the time of the fall of man, that He will continue to perform until this world is subjected to the authority of Jesus Christ. When Jesus Christ rules with a rod of iron, He will restrain sin by the power of the word that proceeds from His mouth. We can thank God that when we were among those who were in the world, the Spirit convicted of sin, the Spirit revealed Jesus Christ as our Righteousness in order that we might have eternal life.

What are we to do with our friends who don't know the gospel, who have never found Jesus Christ as a personal Saviour? Since it is the Spirit's work to reprove and to reveal, does that mean we have no responsibility? No, not at all. God gives us the privilege of presenting the Word of God. We can sow the seed; we can't cause it to germinate, we can't cause it to grow, but we can sow. And when we have sown the Word, our responsibility has ceased, and it is the responsibility of the Spirit of God to water the Word that was sown, to produce His own fruit in His own time. That is why, by every means at our disposal, we will disseminate the Word so that the Spirit of God might take it and use it to bring men to Jesus Christ.

6

THE MIRACLE OF MIRACLES: THE VIRGIN BIRTH OF CHRIST

THE WORD OF GOD ABOUNDS WITH MANIFESTATIONS OF THE greatness of the power of our God. From the opening chapters of Genesis, when by the Word of His mouth this world was brought into being, through to the closing chapters of the Book of the Revelation where we see the creation of the new heavens and the new earth, the pages of the Word abound with evidences that our God is an omnipotent God. There is, perhaps, no miracle that can equal the miracle of the virgin birth of Christ as a manifestation of the omnipotence of God. In our studies of the Person and work of the Holy Spirit, we would like to consider the part that the Holy Spirit played in this miracle of miracles.

From the gospel records which give us the facts concerning the coming of the eternal Son of God in the flesh, we find, first of all, that the Holy Spirit was active in the work of preparation for the coming of Christ. We are not thinking of the preparation in the Old Testament—the preparation through the prophets, the preparation in the inter-advent period—but of the preparation of the persons associated with the coming of Christ. In a previous study we examined something of the relationship of the Holy Spirit to the saints in the Old Testament and we found that certain individuals were given the unique privilege and experience of being filled with the Spirit. There was no promise, as there is today, that all of God's children would be filled with the Spirit. The Holy Spirit sovereignly came upon certain men, at widely different times and at widely different places, to empower them to some ministry. When we consider the birth of Christ, we notice a number of people who had this remarkable experience. That filling of the Spirit was associated with the announcement of a message to the nation Israel that God's promised Messiah had come.

Elisabeth, the mother of John the Baptist, had this unique experience. After the angelic announcement to Mary of the birth of Jesus, Mary journeyed from Galilee, which had been her home, down into the hill country of Judea in the environs of Jerusalem. She "entered into the house of Zacharias, and saluted Elisabeth" Luke (1:40). Then we read: "when Elisabeth heard the salutation of Mary, the babe leaped in her womb; and Elisabeth was filled with the Holy Ghost" (v. 41). Here is an experience such as only a few of the saints in the Old Testament had, as far as Scripture gives any record. The manifestation of this filling with the Holy Spirit was an announcement or a proclamation. The audience that heard it was very small, yet it was an announcement under the control of the Holy Spirit and it is as authoritative as any message delivered by God, the Holy Spirit, in all the Word of God. ". . . she spake out with a loud voice, and said, Blessed art thou among women, and blessed is the fruit of thy womb. And whence is this to me, that the mother of my Lord should come to me?" (v. 42-43).

"My Lord" is a phrase that was lifted out of the Old Testament. David used it as a title for the Lord Jesus Christ, the second Person of the Trinity, who would come into the world as Israel's Messiah. In Psalm 110:1 he says, "The Lord said unto my Lord, Sit thou at my right hand, until I make thine enemies thy footstool." And "my Lord" was a reference to the Messiah who would come to the nation Israel. Elisabeth, controlled by the Holy Spirit, made the announcement that the One who was to be born of Mary was none other than David's greater Son, the Messiah who will redeem Israel, and reign over the nation in fulfillment of God's promises. The angel had told Mary of that same fact (Luke 1:31-33): The One who was to be born of Mary was to "be called the Son of the Highest: and the Lord God shall give unto him the throne of his father David: And he shall reign over the house of Jacob for ever. . . ." Mary had not told Elisabeth what the angel had revealed to her, but the Holy Spirit revealed it.

Zacharias was the second of those associated with the coming of Christ who had this unique experience of being filled with the Spirit: "his father Zacharias was filled with the Holy Ghost, and prophesied . . ." (Luke 1:67). Zacharias, who had been ministering before God as a priest, is given a second ministry by God. He becomes a prophet-priest. In that he is like Ezekiel and Zechariah, men born in the priestly line who also became prophets of God. The ministry of the prophet was to announce a message from God to the people. The message produced by this filling of Zacharias by the Spirit is recorded for us: "Blessed be the Lord God of Israel; for he hath visited and redeemed his people, And hath raised up an horn of salvation for us in the house of his servant David" (v. 68). Further, "That we should be saved from our enemies, and from the hand of all that hate us; To perform the mercy promised to our fathers, and to remember his holy covenant; The oath which he sware to our father Abraham" (vv. 71-73). You will notice that Zechariah mentioned David and Abra-

ham. If you were to look back in the Scriptures you would
find that Matthew (1:1) gives us the relationship of the Lord
Jesus Christ to Abraham and to David. Matthew wants to
prove that Jesus Christ is the Son of Abraham and the Son
of David, because it was to Abraham that God promised a
Blesser, and it was to David that God promised one of his
sons should sit on his throne and reign forever. Abraham
was anticipating a redeemer; David was anticipating one who
would reign. Under the control of the Holy Spirit, Zacharias
says that the One that God promised to Abraham and David
is now to make His advent into the world.

Simeon was the third individual associated with the birth
of Christ who was controlled by the Holy Spirit. Simeon was
a just and devout man. He was waiting for the consolation
of Israel. He was tarrying in the temple, expecting that God's
Messiah would come to God's temple and would bring God's
salvation to God's people. But we read also that "the Holy
Ghost was upon him" (Luke 2:25). This is in the Old Testa-
ment context, and the Old Testament usually refers to the
Spirit coming *upon* a man, rather than by the word *filled*.
Although *filled* is used with reference to Elisabeth and
Zacharias, Simeon had the same experience that they had.
The Spirit came upon Simeon and he was controlled by it.
The result of that control was a message that came by the
Holy Spirit, through Simeon, to the people who were gath-
ered together there. The Holy Ghost had revealed to Simeon
that he should not see death before he had seen the Lord's
Christ, or the Lord's Messiah. The Old Testament promised
that God's Messiah would come to God's temple. Simeon was
waiting for the manifestation of God's Messiah in the place
where God said He would be revealed, and the Holy Spirit
had given this consolation to him. All the Old Testament

saints had hoped that they might live to see Messiah, but Simeon was the only one who had any assurance that he would actually live to see Him. Simeon took the child Jesus into his arms, and he blessed God and said, "Lord, now lettest thou thy servant depart in peace, according to thy word; For mine eyes have seen thy salvation, Which thou hast prepared before the face of all people; A light to lighten the Gentiles, and the glory of thy people Israel" (vv. 29-32). As Simeon took this Babe into his arms and looked down into that face, he said, "mine eyes have seen thy salvation." What a strange way to speak of a child, "thy salvation." But through this One salvation was to be proclaimed. It was to come to Jew and Gentile alike, for salvation would be provided for all men.

These three who were filled with the Spirit are all associated with the birth of Christ. There is one more who was filled with the Holy Spirit, who was related to the presentation of Christ to Israel: An angel made an announcement to Zacharias concerning the birth of John the Baptist. The person and the work of John are described by the angel: "he shall be great in the sight of the Lord, and shall drink neither wine nor strong drink; and he shall be filled with the Holy Ghost, even from his mother's womb" (Luke 1:15). This forerunner, born a few months before Christ was born, was filled with the Holy Spirit from the time of his conception in the womb, and was filled throughout his ministry as he proclaimed and introduced the Lord Jesus Christ. When John stood, at the time that Christ was being presented to the nation Israel, and said, "Behold the Lamb of God, which taketh away the sin of the world" (John 1:29), he was speaking because he was controlled or filled by the Holy Spirit. He was doing the work of a prophet, bringing a message from

God to men. From the Scriptures we find these four people who were peculiarly and uniquely filled with the Holy Spirit, upon whom the Holy Spirit came, whose lips were opened to announce a message, and the message that came forth was the message of a prophet who told the nation Israel that Abraham's Son, David's Son, God's Messiah, the Saviour and Redeemer, had come into this world.

We consider now the work of the Holy Spirit in the miracle of the conception of Christ in the womb of the Virgin Mary. In the first chapter of Matthew's Gospel we are given Joseph's side of this record. Luke was concerned with the events associated with Mary, but Matthew is concerned with the events related to Joseph because he is giving to us the legal relationship of the Lord Jesus Christ to David and Abraham; and legal rights, according to Levitical laws of inheritance, pass from father to son, a father to an adopted son, or a foster father to an adopted son. We read: "Now the birth of Jesus Christ was on this wise: When as his mother Mary was espoused to Joseph, before they came together, she was found with child of the Holy Ghost." (Matthew 1:18). In the angelic announcement to Joseph, the conception of Jesus by the power of the Holy Spirit is asserted.

". . . while he thought on these things, behold, the angel of the Lord appeared unto him in a dream, saying, Joseph, thou son of David, fear not to take unto thee Mary thy wife: for that which is conceived in her is of the Holy Ghost. And she shall bring forth a son, and thou shalt call his name Jesus: for he shall save his people from their sins" (vv. 20-21). Once again the angel affirms the fact that the conception of Jesus was the work of the Holy Spirit. Then again, in response to Mary's natural question, "How shall this be, seeing I know not a man?" the angel answered and said unto her, "The

Holy Ghost shall come upon thee, and the power of the Highest shall overshadow thee: therefore also that holy thing which shall be born of thee shall be called the Son of God" (Luke 1:34-35). For the third time in the Gospel record it is announced that the conception of the Lord Jesus Christ was by the power of the Holy Spirit.

In no place in the Word of God is the Spirit ever referred to as the father of Christ. But if Christ was conceived by the Spirit, why does Scripture not refer to the Spirit as the father of Christ? It is necessary to understand something of the work of each member of the Trinity in this miracle of miracles to be able to answer the question. In Hebrews, we find that God the Father prepared the physical, human body of the Lord Jesus Christ (10:5). Quoting from Psalm 40:6, the author says, "Wherefore when he cometh into the world, he saith, Sacrifice and offering thou wouldest not, but a body hast thou prepared me." The Son, addressing the Father, says that the Father was the active Agent in preparing a body for the eternal Son of God. In Hebrews 2:14 we read: "Forasmuch then as the children are partakers of flesh and blood, he (that is, Jesus Christ) also himself likewise took part of the same; that through death he might destroy him that had the power of death, that is, the devil." When he says, ". . . he . . . took part of the same," the author is talking about a physical body. Thus the passage says that Jesus Christ reached out and took to Himself a physical body which He held in common with all humanity. The Scripture said that the Father prepared the body. The Scripture also said that the Son reached out and appropriated or took the body. The Scripture also says the Holy Spirit conceived the body. How are we going to fit this together? We would conclude that the conception of Jesus was by the Holy Spirit. The life in the One who was conceived was the life of the second Person, the Son of God. The first Person became the Father of the humanity of Jesus Christ. This truly is a mystery. All members of the Godhead worked together to accomplish this miracle, the virgin birth of Jesus Christ. God the Father was the Father of our Lord, according to the flesh. The One who was born was the eternal Son of God, and the life in the womb of the virgin Mary was the life of the eternal Son. The Holy Spirit was the active agent in this conception, so that Christ was conceived by the Holy Ghost and born of the virgin Mary.

It must be pointed out that the miracle was in the conception of Christ, not in the birth of Christ. The birth was a perfectly natural birth. You can go through the passages in Matthew and Luke that deal with the coming of Christ into the world and you will find that what is said of the birth of Christ is that which would be said of any child: Christ was "born" (Matthew 2:1); Christ was "brought forth" (Luke 2:7). Paul tells us that Christ was "made of a woman" (Galations 4:4). These references from the Gospels and Epistles establish the fact that the actual birth of Christ was a natural, normal birth that conformed to all of the laws of birth.

A great many do not believe the record of the Word of God, for they look at this miracle through the eyes of scientific knowledge or rationalistic philosophy and say that the virgin birth is a biological impossibility. They say that the writers of Scripture borrowed some of the pagan mythology of their own days, for Greek and Roman mythology and the mythologies of other peoples who surrounded Palestine had birth narratives relating that gods came from heaven and cohabited with the daughters of men so that children were begotten of those unions. Those children thus conceived, some say, were supernatural beings, above men but below

God. So the unbeliever concludes that these writers of Scripture simply appropriated some heathen mythologies and incorporated them into their records, not knowing that such a thing was impossible. Heathen mythology incorporated the myths concerning the gods dwelling with the daughters of men because God, in the beginning, had revealed the fact that His Saviour was to come by virgin birth, and the knowledge of the coming virgin birth was so widespread that it could not be obliterated. And when men descended into the depths of paganism, even though they repudiated the revelation from God, they were never able to remove the knowledge of the revelation that from the seed of the woman was to come One who would be the Satan-bruiser.

We do not look upon the conception as though the Holy Spirit were an active agent in implanting a sperm to fertilize an ovum within the body of Mary through physical contact. That is not what Luke says. He states, "The Holy Ghost shall come upon thee, and the power of the Highest shall overshadow thee . . ." (Luke 1:35). I call your attention to the word "overshadow." If you go back to the first chapter of the Book of Genesis, you find that "the earth was without form, and void; and darkness was upon the face of the deep." Now, what was the divine process by which order was brought out of this chaos? ". . . the Spirit of God moved upon [or, literally translated, the Spirit of God hovered over, or brooded over] the face of the waters" (v. 2). The Holy Spirit was the active agent in the creation of the earth. He did this by brooding over, or hovering over the earth, not by physical contact. The angel told Mary, "the power of the Highest shall overshadow thee. . . ." This parallel is evident: the Holy Spirit did, in respect to the body of the Lord Jesus Christ, that which He did at the time of the arrangement of

this earth. Out of the substance of the womb of Mary, the
Holy Ghost formed the body of the Lord Jesus Christ. A
miracle was wrought in the womb of the virgin Mary,
whereby the Holy Spirit brought this body which should
be born unto Mary into existence. We must remove from
our thought any pagan idea that the Holy Spirit begat the
humanity of Christ by physical union with Mary. If that be
the case, Christ would have been born by natural conception.

From the Word of God we can see that God was preparing
both the world and the nation Israel for such a miracle. In
the third chapter of the Book of Genesis you find the first
indication of the coming of a Redeemer. The human race
had been plunged into sin by the disobedience of Adam. God
came into the Garden to pronounce a curse upon Satan and
upon the serpent, and the Lord said unto the serpent, "Because thou hast done this, thou art cursed above all cattle,
and above every beast of the field; upon thy belly shalt thou
go, and dust shalt thou eat all the days of thy life: And I
will put enmity [or, I will declare war] between thee [Satan]
and the woman [the willing tool in your hand, the one that
you deceived to accomplish your purpose], and between thy
seed [Satan] and her seed; it [her seed] shall bruise [or
crush] thy head [Satan], and thou shalt bruise his [the seed of
the woman] heel" (vv. 14-15). One can sustain a bruise to
the heel and it does not jeopardize life. One cannot sustain
a bruise to the head without jeopardizing life. The picture
is given here of One who would come into mortal combat
with Satan who has plunged the human race into sin. Satan
would try to strike against the seed of the woman; would,
as it were, put his fangs into the heel of the One that God
would send. But the One that God would send as the seed
of the woman would crush the serpent's head. At the cross

Satan lashed out at the Lord Jesus Christ, and he sank his
fangs into the heel of Christ. Christ put His weight down
onto the head of Satan and crushed him. The cross through
which Satan's head was crushed was the bruising of Christ's
heel. You might ask, "Didn't He die?" Yes, but He died to be
resurrected immediately. No permanent injury, no permanent damage was sustained by Christ; it was the bruising of
His heel. But through the bruising a judgment was pronounced upon Satan. God did not say to Satan, "I will put
enmity between thee and the man, between thy seed and his
seed." Why did He speak of the "seed of the woman"? Because God was preparing for One to be supernaturally conceived and born into this world; One who would be
God-man, who would come into the world by the virgin
birth. This is the first prophecy of the virgin birth of Christ.
   In the prophecy of Isaiah, we find that the little tribe of
Judah is beset by an enemy. The northern kingdom of Israel
has joined in an alliance with Syria, and Syria and Israel
have agreed to march down upon Judah and set up their
puppet king where David's son has the right to rule. The
prophet came to King Ahaz, against whom this threat of
dethronement had been made, and Isaiah announced the
message of God to Ahaz that God would protect him and
that this alliance against him would not succeed. But Ahaz,
a wicked and godless king, did not want God meddling in
his affairs. He did not want to depend upon God for pres-
ervation or protection. And so "the Lord spake again unto
Ahaz, saying, Ask thee a sign of the Lord thy God; ask it
either in the depth, or in the height above" (7:10-11). God
said to Ahaz, "Can it be you don't believe that I can protect
the little nation of Judah from this great alliance? You may
ask Me for any sign you desire; to raise one from the dead,

or to cause the sun to stand still. Ask Me a sign in the heavens above or in the depths beneath." But Ahaz said, "I will not ask, neither will I tempt the Lord" (v. 12). Ahaz did not decline because he was a pious man. Rather, he was forbidding God to give the evidence that He had the power to do what He said He would do. If God has the power to protect Judah, then Judah ought to worship God. But the people loved their idols. So Ahaz said, in effect, "I forbid God to meddle in the affairs of this nation; I won't let Him give me a sign." The prophet replies, "the Lord himself shall give you a sign; Behold, a virgin shall conceive, and bear a son, and shall call his name Immanuel [that is, God with us]. Butter and honey shall he eat, that he may know to refuse the evil, and choose the good. For before the child shall know to refuse the evil, and choose the good, the land that thou abhorrest shall be forsaken of both her kings" (vv. 14-16).

This prophecy had a near view and a far view. The near view revealed that before one could conceive and bear a child, and then wean that child, which would be about two years, both the king of Syria and the king of Israel would be removed from their thrones. In other words, God would depose these two kings in just a few months.

Beyond that near view is this glorious promise that looks forward to the virgin birth of Christ. Matthew records the Holy Spirit's own interpretation of Isaiah 7:14 as we read the angelic announcement: "Now all this was done, that it might be fulfilled which was spoken of the Lord by the prophet, saying, Behold, a virgin shall be with child, and shall bring forth a son, and they shall call his name Emmanuel, which being interpreted is, God with us" (1:22). In the prophecy concerning the seed of the woman, and in the prophecy concerning the virgin who would conceive and bear a child who would have the name "God with us," God the Holy Spirit was preparing for the coming of the Lord Jesus Christ.

We would like to consider, briefly, one more question: Why was it necessary for Jesus Christ to be born of a virgin? Is this a doctrine that we can accept or reject, as we will, or is it necessary? I say to you, on the authority of the Word of God, that if Jesus Christ was not born of a virgin, we have no Saviour at all. If Jesus Christ, the eternal Son of God, came into this world apart from the virgin birth, you and I would not have a Representative who could die for us. In order to understand the necessity for the virgin birth, you must look to the fifth chapter of Hebrews, where the Apostle shows some of the requirements that one must have before he can be a priest: "every high priest taken from among men is ordained for men in things pertaining to God, that he may offer both gifts and sacrifices for sins: Who can have compassion on the ignorant, and on them that are out of the way; for that he himself also is compassed with infirmity" (v. 1). The Apostle says that before one can be a priest to represent man, one must first be a man. If he is not a human being, he is not our representative. If Christ is not one of us, then we have no substitute at all.

"Forasmuch then as the children are partakers of flesh and blood, he also himself likewise took part of the same; that through death he might destroy him that had the power of death, that is, the devil; And deliver them who through fear of death were all their lifetime subject to bondage. For verily he took not on him the nature of angels; but he took on him the seed of Abraham" (Hebrews 2:14-16). Jesus Christ, in order to be the redeemer for men, had to become a man. If He had taken on the nature of angels, for whom would He have died? For angels. But He reached out and took the nature of man. He became flesh, in order that He might represent man. You will remember the law of the kinsman redeemer in the Old Testament: Before one could do the work of a kinsman redeemer, he had to be related to the one who needed redemption. Boaz was able to redeem Ruth because he was a kinsman of Ruth. And the Lord Jesus Christ, in order to redeem you, became what you are: He became man. He did not lay aside His deity, but by this miracle of the virgin birth the eternal Son of God reached out and took to Himself a true humanity so that, as God-man, He might represent us and become our High Priest.

If one is to die for the sins of the world, his death must have infinite value. If the Lord Jesus Christ were only man, He could represent Himself and no others. If one is to die for the sins of the world, there must be sufficient value in his death to cover the sins of the world. And only the infinite and eternal Son of God could offer a sacrifice that would avail for the sins of the whole world from the beginning to the end of time. In the Person of Jesus Christ, and because of the virgin birth, the eternal Son of God became flesh. He was God and Man: Man, in order that He might represent us; God, in order that He might represent all of the claims of the holiness and righteousness and justice of God.

There is one Mediator between God and man; the Man Christ Jesus. Before one can mediate, he has to have contact with the two who are being mediated. If we spoke in different languages, and we wanted to communicate one with the other, it would be necessary to find a mediator or a translator. There is one essential requirement for a translator. He has to know your language and my language; otherwise he could not translate. When the Lord Jesus Christ would redeem sinful men, He came among men in order that He might take our hand into His infinite hand. But, in order to represent the claim of God, He also must be God so that He can put His hand in the hand of the Father. He can unite God and man in Himself because He is God-man.

When we confess Jesus Christ was born of the virgin Mary, we are affirming the truth of the miracle of miracles. The true humanity of the Lord Jesus Christ was conceived in the womb of the virgin by the Holy Spirit, so that He might be our representative before God. Because it was the eternal Son of God who was so born, we who receive Him have the gift of eternal life.

7

RESURRECTION BY THE SPIRIT

THE PREACHING OF THE APOSTLES, AS IT IS RECORDED IN THE Book of Acts, centers around the theme of the resurrection of Jesus Christ from the dead. The great doctrinal portions of the Epistles of the New Testament have the same theme as the basis of the presentation of the truth of God. It was not a new fact that a man should die. From the time of the sin of Adam down to the time of our Lord men had come upon the world's scene to pass, by way of death, from the world. In all of the world's history, as far as we have any record, there were only two men who were removed from the world in any way other than by death. The two, of course, were Enoch and Elijah. Death was the part of all men, therefore it was not something new for the disciples to announce that Christ had died. That which was new and startling, that which authenticated their message as being genuine and a manifestation of divine power, was the announcement that the One who had died had been raised from the dead.

The Apostle Peter mentioned the fact that Jesus Christ, having been "delivered by the determinate counsel and foreknowledge of God, ye have taken, and by wicked hands have crucified and slain" (Acts 2:23). And with that brief notice he seems to pass by the fact of the death of Christ. Not that His death was of little importance, but rather because the value of the death of Christ is evidenced in the resurrection from the dead. Then the Apostle expounds on the doctrine

of resurrection: "Whom God hath raised up . . ."(v. 24). Peter
tells us that the resurrection was a divine work and he asserts the fact that it was God who raised Jesus from the dead
(vv. 24-36). The Apostle does not try to differentiate the Persons in the Trinity and their individual parts in the
resurrection of Christ from the dead. Yet as we go into
the Word of God and consider the subject of the resurrection of Christ, we see that each member of the Godhead
had a particular part in this great act of resurrection.
For instance, in Psalm 16, the resurrection is attributed
to God the Father: "thou wilt not leave my soul in hell;
neither wilt thou suffer thine Holy One to see corruption.
Thou wilt shew me the path of life: in thy presence is fulness
of joy; at thy right hand there are pleasures for evermore"
(vv. 10-11). David, speaking prophetically concerning Jesus
Christ, records that Christ addressed the Father and anticipated that the Father would bring Him to resurrection. Paul
sees the resurrection as the work of the Father. He prays
that they might know "what is the exceeding greatness of
his [the Father's] power to us-ward who believe, according
to the working of his mighty power, Which he [the Father]
wrought in Christ, when he raised him from the dead, and
set him at his own right hand in the heavenly places"
(Ephesians 1:19-20). There the Apostle Paul affirmed the
fact that the resurrection of Jesus Christ was the result of
the work of the Father, as the Father manifested His divine
power and raised His Son from the dead.

   In the Gospel of John, we find our Lord affirms the truth
that the resurrection is the work of the Son Himself. In
this great discourse on the Good Shepherd, explaining the
authority which belongs to Him, Christ said, "No man taketh
it [my life] from me, but I lay it down of myself. I have power

to lay it down, and I have power to take it again. This commandment have I received of my Father" (10:18). The Jews are debating the authority of Jesus Christ. Is He truly the Son of God, or is He a blasphemous impostor? And Christ gives two proofs that He is actually the Son of God who has come with divine approval and authority. The first proof is that He can lay down His life. We recognize the fact that Jesus Christ is the eternal Son of the eternal God. He is the Holy One and a Holy Being is incorruptible; a Holy Being could not see death unless by an act of His own volition he died. It would be impossible for any man to take the life of the Son of God. Jesus Christ received authority from the Father to lay down His life in order that we might have life through His death.

The second great proof of the power and authority of Christ is that "I have power to take it again" (v. 18). Here the Son is affirming that He, after He has laid down His life, will come forth from the grave triumphant over death.

The resurrection may be also attributed to the work of the Holy Spirit as well as to the work of the Father and the Son. Paul says he has the right to call Jesus Christ "God's Son" because He was "declared to be the Son of God with power, according to the spirit of holiness, by the resurrection [of Jesus Christ] from the dead" (Romans 1:4). Among Bible students, there are two different interpretations of this phrase, "the spirit of holiness." Many good Bible teachers believe that this refers to the essential spirit of the Lord Jesus Christ, that He is the Holy One, and because He is the Holy One it was impossible that He could continue in the state of death. By an act of His will He might dismiss His soul from His body and He might lay down His life as a ransom for the sins of the world. But He was resurrected because it was not possible that He should be held by death. The phrase, "the spirit of holiness" may refer to the spirit of Christ Himself. We would suggest, however, that this also may have reference to the Third Person of the Trinity, the Holy Spirit. Thus the Apostle may be affirming the truth that the Holy Spirit operated in the resurrection of Jesus Christ to present this world with incontrovertible evidence that Jesus Christ, although rejected by His own people and prevented from coming to His own things, is actually the Son of God. The Holy Spirit so operated with the Father and the Son, that the Triune God was active in the work of resurrection.

The Apostle also says, "But if the Spirit of him that raised up Jesus from the dead dwell in you, he that raised up Christ from the dead shall also quicken [or make alive] your mortal bodies by his Spirit that dwelleth in you" (Romans 8:11). Now this seems to be quite a clear reference to the work of the Third Person. The Holy Spirit was the active agent in bringing Jesus Christ from the dead, and Paul so affirms that the Spirit who dwells in us and quickens us was the same Spirit who operated in Jesus Christ to bring Him forth from the grave.

A third reference is found in I Peter, where once again we have a passage that is interpreted in two different ways by Bible students: "For Christ also hath once suffered for sins, the just for the unjust, that he might bring us to God, being put to death in the flesh, but quickened by the Spirit (3:18). There are some who feel that the Spirit in this verse should be written with a small "s," to support the teaching that Christ was quickened in His spirit, and it would be in keeping with the passage to contrast the flesh and the spirit. However, there is good reason for believing that it should be understood as it is written in your text, with a

capital "S," teaching that Christ was put to death in the flesh
in order that He might represent all who were born in the
flesh and are under sin, but that He was quickened, or made
alive, by the work of the Holy Spirit of God. This would
be a third affirmation of the fact that the Triune God was
active in this work of resurrection.

Perhaps it is a little mystifying to comprehend how Christ
could be raised by the Father, could raise Himself, and also
be raised by the Spirit at the same time. We are face to face
with one of the great mysteries of the Word of God, one
which we cannot fathom with our finite minds. Scripture
says, "In the beginning God created the heaven and the
earth" (Genesis 1:1). John tells us, "All things were made
by him" (1:3); that is, by the Son. The Spirit was also the
active agent in creation, according to the Word of God. We
saw, in our study concerning the virgin birth, that the
Father gave the Son, that the Son gave Himself and took
to Himself humanity, and that the Spirit was also the active
agent in the virgin birth of Christ. In the great plan of
redemption, redemption was designed and planned by the
Father, purchased by the Son, and is applied to those who
are God's own by the work of the Holy Spirit. In the work
of inspiration of Scripture, which we attribute to the Holy
Spirit, it is the truth of the Father that is revealed. The Son
is the Person revealed so that He might reveal the Father,
and the Spirit is the agent who does the revealing. This is
also true in the resurrection of Jesus Christ. I would question
whether there is any great work of God revealed in the
Word of God in which all of the members of the Godhead
do not work together to accomplish God's purpose and design. I do not know that we can say any one thing is the work
of the Father, and another thing the work of the Son, and

relegate to some other sphere the work of the Spirit. Together they accomplish the work.

The Apostle Paul uses a particular Greek word to emphasize the divine power manifested in the resurrection of Christ; it is the Greek word *dunamis,* from which we get our English word, "dynamite," which inadequately conveys the sense of the original word. *Dunamis,* in the original language, refers not to some external explosive force, powerful as that might be, but to the power that is inherent in a thing itself. We talk about the gospel as the "power of God." We sometimes refer to the gospel as the "dynamite of God." If you want to put it in graphic words, don't use "dynamite." Use "atomic energy," because atomic energy is the release of the power that is inherent in a thing itself. And when the Apostle speaks of the power of God that was operative in the resurrection of Christ, he is referring to the intrinsic, omnipotence of God the Father (Ephesians 1:19-20).

In John 10:18, where Christ speaks of His part in the resurrection, the English text says, "I have power to lay it down, and I have power to take it again." You would not learn from that translation that Christ used an entirely different Greek word from that used in Ephesians 1. The word translated "power" in John 10:18 is the Greek word for "authority" or "right." And Christ is saying, "No man takes my life from me; I lay it down of myself. I have the right to lay it down and I have the right, or the authority, to take it up again." Christ is saying that God gave to the Son certain rights, and the power of God was not manifested apart from the rights or the authority that belonged to the Second Person of the Godhead. It was the power of God that raised Christ, but it was by the authority of the Son that He was raised. Yet the Holy Spirit was the active agent,

working in harmony with the authority of the Son, to release
the power of God so that Jesus Christ could be brought from
the grave. Jesus Christ not only had the power to come forth
from the grave, He had the perfect right to come forth because He was the Holy One, He was the Son of God, who had
given His life as the ransom for many. Salvation was finished
and God could hold Him in the bonds of death no longer.

In the Gospel of Matthew we have the record of the sealing
of the tomb and the assigning of the guard to watch the
tomb: "Now the next day, that followed the day of preparation, the chief priests and Pharisees came together unto
Pilate, Saying, Sir, we remember that deceiver said, while
he was yet alive, After three days I will rise again" (27:62-63).
Obviously the unbelievers who had listened to Christ preach
retained more of His teaching about the resurrection than
did the disciples, for the disciples were nonplussed when
word was brought to them that Christ had been resurrected.
But the unbelievers remembered that Jesus had promised
that He would rise and were taking measures to prevent it:
"Command therefore that the sepulchre be made sure until
the third day, lest his disciples come by night, and steal him
away, and say unto the people, He is risen from the dead: so
the last error shall be worse than the first. Pilate said unto
them, Ye have a watch: go your way, make it as sure as ye
can. So they went, and made the sepulchre sure, sealing the
stone, and setting a watch" (27:64-66).

They sealed the stone and they set a watch to prevent any
acts which might be used by the disciples to prove His power
and authority. The seal was a sign of the authority of Rome
and the guard a display of the power of Rome. But Christ, by
His resurrection, showed that He had rights that exceeded
the authority of Rome, and power that exceeded the might

of Rome. You will remember that when the soldiers came to arrest Christ, He spoke a word and those soldiers fell to the ground. The original text suggests that they were pinned to the ground. Unless Christ had released that manifestation of His power, they never could have gotten up to arrest Him. Here are soldiers in whom a duplicate evidence of the power of Christ is manifested. The armed guards at the tomb could not prevent Him from coming forth from the grave.

Notice a second thing in Matthew's record: "there was a great earthquake: for the angel of the Lord descended from heaven, and came and rolled back the stone from the door, and sat upon it" (28:2). The angel from heaven obviously had a right that exceeded the right and authority of the Roman government whose seal was upon that tomb. Jesus Christ, by His resurrection, was manifesting the same divine power and authority of God.

The resurrection of Jesus Christ has two very important applications for us. We have a promise that has great practical value because of the assurance it brings our own hearts. Paul said, ". . . if the Spirit of him that raised up Jesus from the dead dwell in you [and it most certainly does!], he that raised up Christ from the dead shall also quicken your mortal bodies by his Spirit that dwelleth in you" (Romans 8:11). The word "quicken" means "to make alive" and Paul refers to the nature of this body which we possess. It is a mortal body, a body which is subject to death; a body which, unless the Lord Jesus comes to translate us into His presence, will be reduced to dust from which it was originally taken. Yet the very Spirit that resurrected Jesus Christ has been given to us as our possession, and the Spirit who was operative in releasing the power of God in the body of Jesus Christ to bring it to resurrection will do for us exactly what He did for the

Lord Jesus Christ. The body of the Lord Jesus Christ saw no corruption. The Psalmist told us that fact: "thou wilt not . . . suffer thine Holy One to see corruption" (Psalm 16:10). Jesus Christ was in the grave sufficient time for corruption to have set in, but His body did not see corruption. Even though the Spirit will not preserve our bodies from corruption, that does not mean that He will not do for us what He did for the Lord Jesus Christ. He will bring this body, which is now a mortal body, out of the grave, complete and perfect, and it will become an immortal body. That is why the Apostle Paul says, ". . . this mortal must put on immortality" (I Corinthians 15:53). Paul is not talking about the soul; he is talking about the body. This mortal body must put on immortality and this corruptible body must put on incorruption. The power of God, on the basis of the authority of Jesus Christ, released through the Holy Spirit, will do for believers what the Spirit did for the Lord Jesus Christ on the resurrection morning so many years ago.

The Apostle reveals that the Holy Spirit has been given to indwell us not only to bring these bodies to resurrection, but to produce a new kind of life in us while we are awaiting our transformation into His presence. The Apostle is concerned for his children in the Lord, and after he has presented the great doctrinal truths he addresses God in prayer on their behalf. He wants them to know something that they didn't really know yet, and he prays, "The eyes of your understanding being enlightened; that ye may know . . ." (Ephesians 1:18). He wants them to know the hope of His calling and the riches of the glory of God's inheritance in the saints. He wants them to know what is the exceeding greatness of God's power to us who believe. And here, the Apostle brings us face to face with this stupendous fact that the same power that was manifested in bringing Jesus Christ from the grave is a power that is resident within us, that can operate through us to produce a new life as effectively as it produced a resurrection in the body of the Lord Jesus Christ. He wants us to know the "exceeding greatness of his power to us-ward who believe, according to the working of his mighty power, Which he wrought in Christ, when he raised him from the dead . . ." (1:19-20)—"You . . . , who were dead in trespasses and sins" (2:1). When we affirm the fact, as we have in previous studies, and will in subsequent studies, that the Holy Spirit has been given to indwell the child of God, we are affirming the truth that God has put within us the power of God which brought Jesus Christ from the dead. It is not a latent power, not a static force, but a power that is vital and living, one which is seeking to manifest itself through us.

We have been united with Christ in His death, in His burial and in His resurrection. ". . . we are buried with him by baptism into death: that like as Christ was raised up from the dead by the glory of the Father, even so we also should walk in newness of life" (Romans 6:4). When Jesus Christ stepped forth from the grave, He was walking a new kind of life. It was not a sinless life as opposed to a sinful life, for there was no sin in our Lord before His resurrection. But Jesus Christ was possessed of a new, glorified body; He was realizing the answer to His prayer that God would give Him the glory that was His and which He had with the Father from eternity.

We see ourselves under the curse of God because of sin, but that penalty upon sin has been executed and we are therefore justified. We are free from the penalty of sin because that penalty has been executed in the Person of Jesus Christ. And we are resurrected with Christ so that, by the Spirit's power, we might walk in newness of life. As Christ was raised by the glory of the Father, so that He might manifest forth the glory of the Father, so we have been resurrected that we might manifest forth the glory of God. God the Father sees us not as we are in our experience, but as perfect in Christ. He sees us as having died; He sees us as having been resurrected; He sees us as having ascended and being seated at the right hand of the Father, in glory. To the Father, we are His glorious sons. The hope of God's calling is that many sons might be brought into glory, and in the eyes of God that is an accomplished fact. The truth of the resurrection of Christ gives us the basis for believing that we will be brought, as glorious ones, into His presence at our resurrection. The resurrection of Jesus Christ means that you and I can live today a resurrection kind of life. That is why the Apostle writes to the Galatians and says that if we walk according to the flesh, we will fulfill the lusts of the flesh, but if we are walking by means of the Holy Spirit, the Spirit will produce His own righteousness in us.

Our Lord, after the miracle of feeding the five thousand, wanted to tell those who had been fed that He had come to give them the bread from heaven. As Moses gave them the manna in the wilderness, even so the Father gives them the true bread from heaven. Then the Son began to describe that bread that He came to give and the kind of life that He came to impart: "I am the bread of life: he that cometh to me shall never hunger; and he that believeth on me shall never thirst" (John 6:35). There will be complete satisfaction, because every need is met as one partakes of the life that the Lord Jesus Christ gives. We see that the life which Christ gives is resurrection life: "this is the Father's will which hath sent me, that of all which he hath given me I should lose nothing, but should raise it up again at the last day. And this is the will of him that sent me, that every one which seeth the Son, and believeth on him, may have everlasting life: and I will raise him up at the last day" (vv. 39-40). It is a satisfying life, an everlasting life; it is resurrection life.

The Lord Jesus Christ was not looking forward to the completion of His program when believers would be brought into His presence. He was thinking of the present experience of the children of God. He says that we partake of the life of Christ today. That is why the child of God is exhorted to live daily by the power of the Spirit of God so that the truth of the resurrection may not be just that to which we give assent, but that which we translate into living by walking in the newness of life.

8

THE ADVENT OF THE SPIRIT

A FEW DAYS AGO A SALESMAN WAS TALKING WITH ME, TRYING
to interest me in a certain product. In the course of the conversation he asked my name and I told him it was Pentecost.
He looked at me and said, "What did you say?" I repeated,
"Pentecost." He stammered, "Like—uh—like in the Bible?"
I replied, "Yes, like in the Bible." He said, "You know, I've
heard people talk about that name, and I know it is something very important, but I never did know what it was."

There are many of God's children who have heard of the
day of Pentecost and yet they are quite in the dark as to the
significance of that momentous event. In our studies on
the Person and work of the Spirit, we have given attention to
the work of the Holy Spirit in the Old Testament and the
work of the Holy Spirit in reference to the world in general.
We have also spoken of the ministry of the Holy Spirit in relation to the Person of the Lord Jesus Christ. We are now
moving into an area of study that is of utmost importance to
the child of God, for we will be considering the ministry
of the Holy Spirit to the believer. We will consider the part
that the Holy Spirit plays in bringing us to a new birth; His
work of uniting us to Jesus Christ; His work of empowering
us; His work of filling us, all of which so vitally affect our
lives.

Those who have studied the Word of God realize that the
ministries of the Holy Spirit to the believer began, histori-

cally, on the day of Pentecost. We come time and time again to the second chapter of the Book of Acts in order that we might read the record of His advent into the world. When we talk of the advent of the Spirit we have to be careful about the term we use, for we have seen that there never was a time when the Holy Spirit was not resident in the world. The Holy Spirit, as the omnipresent member of the Triune Godhead never was absent or away from the world, and yet He came to dwell in a unique way on the day of Pentecost.

Luke tells us that "when the day of Pentecost was fully come, they [that is, the one hundred and twenty believers who assembled in the upper room] were all with one accord in one place" (Acts 2:1). And as these believers were gathered together, there came a manifestation of the Spirit's presence among them. It was audible to the ear as well as visible to the eye. There came "a sound from heaven as of a rushing mighty wind . . ." (v. 2), so that none of those gathered together was in ignorance that something was taking place. There "appeared unto them cloven tongues like as of fire, and it sat upon each of them" (v. 3). The advent of Christ was real because He could be seen, felt and heard. Luke is bearing testimony to the reality of the advent of the Spirit. This is not a deception in the minds of men, but an actual, historical event that could be attested to by a large number of witnesses.

It is very significant that the advent took place when the day of Pentecost was "fully come." In order to understand this we will have to go back to the Old Testament. The Passover was instituted the night God delivered the children of Israel out of Egypt. God had given nine plagues which came upon the Egyptians. Finally, God announced a tenth plague, the result of which would cause Pharaoh to release the people from their bondage. The Israelites were commanded to place the blood of a sacrifice upon the side posts and the top of the door, and God promised that when He saw the blood, He would pass over them, or, as it might literally be translated, He would hover over them. The Spirit of God hovered over every home upon whose door posts the blood had been applied to prevent the death angel from entering. The Passover was then observed every year as a memorial to God's deliverance and God's protection (Leviticus 23:5). Paul tells us that "Christ our passover is sacrificed for us" (I Corinthians 5:7), and as we put Leviticus 23 alongside these words we can see that what took place in the Old Testament anticipated an event in the New Testament: the Lord Jesus Christ, as the Lamb of God, shed His blood that we might come under the covering of His blood and that He might hover over us to protect us and keep us as His own blood-bought ones.

The feast of the Unleavened Bread followed the Passover. The ones who observed the Passover, and feasted upon the Passover lamb, were to observe a seven-day period in which there was no leaven in their homes. Those who had partaken of the Passover lamb were to be separated from the leaven, the sign of uncleanness. In I Corinthians 5:7 believers are exhorted to "Purge out therefore the old leaven. . . ." A new kind of life was to characterize them.

The third feast described in the Old Testament is the feast of the First Fruits. When the children of Israel came into the land and reaped the bounty which God gave them, they were to gather together some of the sheaves of that harvest and wave the sheaves before the Lord. In the New Testament you find that Christ is the first fruits (I Corinthians 15:23). He is the first fruits of many who will follow Him in the harvest because of His resurrection. You will notice that God has instituted these feasts according to a pre-arranged plan. Christ, who is our Passover, redeems by blood and brings those who are saved into a new kind of life; Christ, who is the wave-sheaf, is the first fruits of the harvest that will be brought to God by His resurrection. So, you have Christ crucified and Christ resurrected represented in these feasts.

The feast of Pentecost follows fifty days after the Passover (Leviticus 23:15-22). Pentecost means "fifty days later." Moses was told on the fiftieth day, "ye shall offer a new meat offering unto the Lord. Ye shall bring out of your habitations two wave loaves . . ." (vv. 16-17). The children of Israel who had passed through the harvest of the first fruits were to take the wheat of that harvest and grind it into flour, and bake the flour into bread. Then they were to offer that bread to God. The offering on this second thanksgiving service was not one of sheaves, but rather of loaves—that which had been unified, put together and then offered to God. This feast showed us that through the death and the resurrection of Christ, there was to come a great harvest to God.

In the New Testament, specific reference is made to the relation of Jesus Christ to these feasts. He is our Passover who has been sacrificed for us. We are to observe a new kind of life, a life without leaven, because we belong to Him. By His resurrection He promises us a resurrection like unto His and when we see Him we shall be like Him for we shall see Him as He is. But, when we come to the feast of Pentecost, we are moving into the realm of the Holy Spirit, for He will be the agent who will unite the people and present them to God. The Old Testament anticipated that this work would be accomplished in the millennial age when Jesus Christ would come to this earth and institute His kingdom. Then the Holy Spirit would be poured out upon all flesh at which time He would do His work of gathering together a loaf that would be offered to God as God's harvest of the earth. The Old Testament never anticipated that the Lord Jesus Christ would come and present Himself as a king, that He would be rejected as a king by Israel; and that God would turn to a new people, and from among Jews and Gentiles would gather together a loaf that would be offered to God before the loaf out of Israel would be offered when the King instituted His kingdom. When the Jews of the Old Testament celebrated the day of Pentecost, they were looking forward to the time when the harvest would be completed and the people of God would be brought together to be united by the Spirit.

The closing chapters of the four Gospels record the most unique Passover in Israel's history. All Jewish Passovers were observed by the slaying of a lamb. But here we have God's Passover, when God offered a Lamb to take away the sin of the world. The blood that was shed was not the blood of an animal, but the blood of the infinite and eternal Son of God. The believers had witnessed His resurrection, the fulfillment of the wave-sheaf. They had heard Him say, ". . . tarry ye in the city of Jerusalem, until ye be endued with power from on high" (Luke 24:49). If you were to go back into John's Gospel, you would see that the Son said that when He had ascended unto the Father He would ask the Father and the Father would send them the Holy Spirit. This was to be the fulfillment of the feast of Pentecost. These believers had gone through a season of feasts and observances of such significance they could scarcely grasp them. The Passover Lamb had been sacrificed; the wave-sheaf (Jesus Christ alive from the dead) had been presented before them as the first fruits.

There is yet one more significant feast that must be fulfilled before this cycle is complete. The wave-loaf must be offered on the day of Pentecost. As this feast had fully come, and they were all in one accord in one place, there was a manifestation that the Spirit of God had come to fulfill all anticipated in this feast.

To understand what took place in the upper room, we must go back to the events preceding the erection of the tabernacle in the wilderness. God took Moses up on the mountain and gave him specific instructions as to how the tabernacle was to be built. The coverings, curtains, boards, supports—all of the articles of furniture—were revealed to Moses in detail. And Moses was provided with gifted craftsmen to build the tabernacle according to the divine plan. But, even though carefully planned and intricately executed, it was just an empty tent until a most significant event took place: "Then a cloud covered the tent of the congregation, and the glory of the Lord filled the tabernacle. And Moses was not able to enter into the tent of the congregation, because the cloud abode thereon, and the glory of the Lord filled the tabernacle" (Exodus 40:34-35). That tent was transformed into a place from which the presence of God was manifested because the glory of God came and filled it. You see the same thing again when Solomon erected the temple which was to be the meeting place between God and man after the tabernacle had outlived its usefulness. Solomon erected a temple that was perhaps the most splendid and glorious edifice the world has ever seen. But it was only an empty building, in spite of its costly stones and its adornments of gold, until, on the day of dedication, "the glory of the Lord had filled the house . . ." (I Kings 8:11). And the temple was transformed from a beautifully ornameted building to that place from which God manifested Himself when the Shekinah glory of God moved in.

In the New Testament, God is choosing a new temple. It is not a temple to be made from the skins of animals, as was the tabernacle; nor was it to be erected out of hewn stones, overlaid with gold, as was the temple; it was to be built, Peter tells us, out of living stones—the believers in the Lord Jesus Christ.

The Holy Spirit, on the day of Pentecost, came to construct and indwell the temple of God. At the moment this building was first constructed, it seems to have had only one hundred and twenty stones. It was small; unattractive when measured by man's standards; insignificant and despised by those who frequented the old temple. Yet, when the Holy Spirit of God came into the world and moved into that temple, transforming it by His presence, it became the place of divine manifestation. Just as the Shekinah glory of God transformed the tabernacle and the temple when they were dedicated to Him, so, on the day of Pentecost, the Holy Spirit came into believers who had been united by the Spirit with Christ to possess that building as His edifice and to dwell there.

Paul tells us, "What? know ye not that your body is the temple of the Holy Ghost . . . ?" (I Corinthians 6:19). How does your body become the temple? Because the Spirit of God moved in and took up residence in your body when you accepted Christ as Saviour. Not only are believers individually indwelt, but all believers, corporately, are indwelt by the Holy Spirit: "In whom all the building fitly framed together groweth unto an holy temple in the Lord: In whom ye also are builded together for an habitation of God through the Spirit" (Ephesians 2:21-22). Paul explains exactly what happened in Acts 2. Here was a body; it was to become a temple of God; it was an empty shell, as empty as the tabernacle or the temple, until the Holy Spirit of God came to take up residence in it and transform it. That which has been dead has become a living temple, indwelt by the Spirit of God.

When Luke tells us (Acts 2:3) that there appeared to the believers cloven tongues, like fire, that sat upon each of them, this has reference to what Moses reported he saw in the tabernacle—the Shekinah glory of God that filled the tabernacle. It is the same thing that Solomon recorded when the priests saw the glory of God. These tongues of fire were none other than a manifestation of that glory which had not been seen since Ezekiel's day when it departed from the temple because of the idolatry and the apostasy practiced in that building which had previously been set forth to the use of God. On the day of Pentecost a temple is being formed. It is to be set apart for God's use. It must, therefore, be occupied and indwelt by God. God, the Holy Spirit, came to form and indwell the temple. They heard the sound of His coming, and they saw this visible manifestation of the glory of God.

Following the manifestation, there was a demonstration to the world that God had come to possess His temple: "they were all filled with the Holy Ghost, and began to speak with other tongues, as the Spirit gave them utterance" (Acts 2:4). Here again is a parallel, for when Moses erected the tabernacle and the Shekinah glory of God came to fill that tabernacle, it was immediately demonstrable that something had happened. Those who went into the tabernacle saw the glory of God. When God moved into the temple Solomon erected, it was immediately demonstrable because men could see the glory of God. When we read, "they were all filled . . . ," this refers to both individual and corporate indwelling. As a group they were indwelt by the Holy Spirit: they became God's temple. Individually they were filled or controlled by the Holy Spirit, and each spoke as the Spirit gave him utterance.

All those in Jerusalem who had come together to the feast of Pentecost soon heard what happened in the upper room, for that which took place among these hundred and twenty could not be hidden: "this was noised abroad . . ." (v. 6). When the multitude came together they were confounded. The demonstration was the power given to these disciples to speak in other languages the wonderful works of God, so that these hearers could understand exactly what had happened. These people came from many different countries, yet each heard the disciples speak in his own tongue. This was no ecstatic utterance addressed to God by way of worship. This was a miracle: "every man heard them speak in his own language" (v. 6); "hear we every man in our own tongue . . ." (v. 8); "we do hear them speak in our tongues the wonderful works of God" (v. 11). There was a double miracle: a miracle in the speaking and a miracle in the hearing.

Such a manifestation demands an explanation. It could be a natural phenomenon or a supernatural phenomenon. A natural phenomenon could be explained by saying that these men were controlled by wine; a supernatural or supranatural phenomenon would mean they were controlled by either God or Satan. When the Jews heard them speak, they had their explanation. They said it was a natural phenomenon; that these men were full of new wine; they were intoxicated. Now this word "new wine" can be variously interpreted. It is the word normally used for freshly pressed grape juice, which was not fermented at all. It seems as though these men were giving one of the strongest slurs that they knew, for they said, "These men are so naive, such babes in the woods, that they have taken a nip of grape juice and it has set them ranting and raving." They saw no manifestation of divine power in it, but a drunken man does not speak the wonderful works of God. Oh, the deception in their minds as they attributed to alcohol that which was produced by the Spirit of God!

Peter denies that they were controlled by spirits, but rather, he says, they are controlled by the Spirit: "these are not drunken, as ye suppose, seeing it is but the third hour of the day" (Acts 3:15). The day of Pentecost was a feast day and, according to the law, they could not touch any intoxicating beverage during the day of the feast. The last wine they could have touched would have been before sundown the day before. The effects of anything they might have had before sundown the night before would have worn off before nine o'clock in the morning. As good Jews they would not be permitted to touch any more wine until sundown that night. Since they are halfway between, Peter shows that it was impossible for them to be controlled by wine.

What, then, is the explanation? Peter tells us, ". . . this is that which was spoken by the prophet Joel" (Acts 2:16). He quotes the extended passage from Joel 2, where Joel prophesies that following the events of the great tribulation, when the sun shall be darkened and the moon shall be turned to blood, during the judgments of the day of the Lord upon the earth before the second advent of Jesus Christ to the earth, men will cry out for some knowledge of God and will not find Him because of the hardness and impenitence of their hearts (vv. 17-20). But after the judgments of the day of the Lord, or the tribulation, are over, the Son of God will come and the Spirit of God will be poured out on all flesh. Then there will be a revelation of truth which they formerly were unable to receive because they had no one to reveal the truth to them.

Joel promised that the Spirit of God would be given to the nation Israel at the second advent of Messiah to the earth. He was anticipating the fulfillment of the feast of Pentecost. There would be a Passover; Christ would be sacrificed. There would be the first fruits; Christ would be resurrected. The Spirit would come so that He could gather together the loaf that would be offered to God. Joel was not anticipating the formation of the church; that was a mystery not revealed in the Old Testament.

The miracle of declaring the wonderful works of God so that each man heard in his own tongue is an authentication that this is supernatural power. The explanation is that God, who gave the Passover Lamb, has fulfilled not only the feast of Passover, and the feast of First Fruits, but also He has now fulfilled what was anticipated in the feast of Pentecost.

What does this mean to us? What does it mean that the Holy Spirit has come? Christ has said, "I will pray the Father, and he shall give you another Comforter, that he may abide with you for ever" (John 14:16). "Jesus answered and said unto him, If a man love me, he will keep my words: and my Father will love him, and we will come unto him, and make our abode with him" (v. 23). We will come *unto* him and make our abode *with* him. Our Lord was anticipating what was historically accomplished on the day of Pentecost: God the Father, God the Son, and God the Holy Spirit came to take up residence in the body of believers and in every believer in the Lord Jesus Christ. This word has been fulfilled: "ye in me, and I in you" (John 14:20). We are in

Christ and Christ is in us. We are in the Father and the Father is in us. We are in the Spirit and the Spirit is in us. "Ye are the temple of the Holy Ghost"; "ye in me and I in you."

When God came to dwell in Solomon's temple He dwelt in a building that was the architectural marvel of the whole world. Yet the glory of the temple was not in its materials, but in the fact that Jehovah dwelt there. And the building in which He dwells today is the architectural marvel of all heaven, for it is composed of "living stones," made of sinners who have been redeemed and cleansed. Yet the glory of this new temple is that God dwells there.

9

THE SPIRIT AND REGENERATION

THERE IS A VERY CLOSE PARALLEL BETWEEN THE TRUTH PRE-
sented in the first chapter of Genesis and the truth presented
in the first chapter of John's Gospel. In Genesis we have the
ministry of the Holy Spirit in generation, and in John we
have the work of the Holy Spirit in regeneration.

In the first chapter of Genesis the announcement is made
that this material earth came into existence by the spoken
Word of God. All that has material substance was brought
into being out of nothing as God manifested the greatness of
His power by calling this vast universe into existence. And
this work of God is further explained when we learn that
there was a time when the earth was devoid of life, "without
form, and void . . ." (Genesis 2:2). While in that state, darkness was upon the face of the deep.

It is at that point that we are introduced to the ministry
of the Holy Spirit, the agent in creation, who took a place
above and superior to the formless earth, and began to move
or to hover over the earth, so that because of His motion,
locomotion began on the earth: "the Spirit of God moved
upon the face of the waters" (v. 2). The word "moved" could
be translated "brooded." It is the word that would be used
to describe a hen sitting on eggs. There are many who feel
that this is the import of the word. They say that heathen
mythology abounds with narratives of creation which state
that life came out of an egg. Many unbelievers say that

the writer of the Book of Genesis adopted heathen mythology and, because life comes out of that which manifests no life, somehow life came out of no life because of this brooding of the Holy Spirit.

There is another meaning in this word which will enlarge our conception. In Deuteronomy 32, Moses is reviewing God's dealing with the nation Israel. He is extolling God for His faithfulness and calling the children of Israel to faithfulness because of what God has done. Moses uses a number of different figures to show how faithful God has been as a preserver. "He is the Rock . . ." (v. 4); One in whom they can hide, a fortress and shelter in any time of storm. God is the One who gave them the land of Palestine as their inheritance and drove out the enemy before Him (v. 8). "As an eagle stirreth up her nest, fluttereth over her young, spreadeth abroad her wings, taketh them, beareth them on her wings: So the Lord alone did lead him [Jacob], and there was no strange god with him" (vv. 11-12).

Moses is referring to the phenomenon in which an eagle will hover over her young until it has come time for her to abandon the nest. If the eaglet is not compelled to fly, it would never venture out of the nest and would be nestbound. The eagle watches over her young until such a time as they are able to begin to fly and then she "fluttereth over her young." This word "fluttereth" is the word used back in Genesis 1:2, and translated "moved." It suggests that the eagle, who has been hovering and protecting, now comes down and nudges those fledglings who want to stay in the nest. The mother eagle stands on the edge of the nest and she begins to nudge, to move, to stir up the nest. And those fledglings, who were perfectly content, are nudged into action. Will you notice that this word has nothing to do with

hatching the egg; it has nothing to do with sitting on the nest
so that life is produced and made visible; rather, the mother
eagle nudges into motion. That is the meaning of Genesis
1:2. The Spirit of God hovered over the earth and produced
life where there had been only material substance.

God said, "Let there be light . . ." (Genesis 1:3). Again,
God said, "Let there be a firmament in the midst of the
waters . . ." (v. 6). Then God said, "Let the waters under
the heaven be gathered together unto one place, and let the
dry land appear: and it was so" (v. 9). And God said, "Let
there be lights in the firmament of the heaven to divide the
day from the night . . ." (v. 14). Observe that in these first
four creative days God called something into existence simply
by saying, "Let it be." It is on the fifth day that life manifests
itself because these immaterial things were nudged into
action, or were vivified, by the work of the Holy Spirit. God
said, "Let the waters bring forth abundantly the moving
creature that hath life . . ." (v. 20). He didn't say, "Let
there *be* living creatures on the earth." He said, "Let that
which is material and lifeless bring forth life." It was not the
lifeless ooze that suddenly brought forth life so that material
creation was vivified by the immaterial or lifeless creation,
as the evolutionists would suggest. But the Spirit of God
began to vivify that which was lifeless and produced life out
of it. God said, "Let the earth bring forth the living creature
after his kind . . ." (v. 24). Again, God did not say, "Let
there *be* living creatures on the earth." The Spirit of God
was "moving" to bring life on the earth. And God said, "Let
us make man in our image, after our likeness . . ." (v. 26).
During the last three creative days, the Holy Spirit was truly
doing His work of vivifying. God produced material things
by the Word of His mouth, but life was called out of this
material creation by the work of the Holy Spirit of God.

God said, "of the tree of the knowledge of good and evil, thou shalt not eat of it: for in the day that thou eatest thereof thou shalt surely die" (Genesis 2:17). Man possessed physical life after the fall, but he had no more spiritual life than the earth had before God caused the Holy Spirit to vivify it and produce life upon it. The Holy Spirit, in regeneration, is dealing with something that is utterly lifeless and devoid of spiritual life. That is what the Apostle Paul meant when he said, "And you hath he quickened, who were dead . . ." (Ephesians 2:1). A sinner needs the Holy Spirit to take what is dead and devoid of life and make it alive.

When the Holy Spirit does His work in the new birth, or regeneration, He relates us to a Person. There is no life apart from a person and the gift of eternal life centers in the Person of Jesus Christ. The Word of God teaches that a man receives life by receiving Jesus Christ as Saviour. That is why our Lord said, "I am the way, the truth, and the life . . ." (John 14:6). He did not say, "I *have* the way, the truth, and the life," as though it were a gift that He could dispense, as though He were simply the agent who gave eternal life. Do you remember what our Lord said, after He had worked the miracle of feeding the five thousand? "I am the bread of life . . ." (John 6:35). He didn't say, "I *have* the bread of life, and anyone who wants it can come and get it from me." After raising Lazarus from the dead, Christ said, "I am the resurrection, and the life . . ." (John 11:25); not, "I *have* life to impart." This brings home to us the fact that if we are to have life, we must have Jesus Christ. Since Jesus Christ is the life, the Spirit must bring us into a living, vital union with Him.

How does the Holy Spirit vivify or make one alive in Christ? Paul did not say, "If any man accepts a gift *from* Christ," but "if any men be *in* Christ, he is a new creature

. . ." (II Corinthians 5:17). The marginal reading in this text
is not "he is a new creature," but "he is a new creation." Now
why does Paul talk about us as a new creation? Because the
Spirit of God does for the sinner who is dead in trespasses
and sins exactly what He did for creation that was dead and
devoid of life. As the Holy Spirit vivified creation, so that it
could bring forth after its kind and manifest life, the Spirit
of God produces a new birth that gives us a new life, and
the new life is Jesus Christ Himself. What has happened?
". . . old things are passed away . . ." (5:17). What are the old
things? Spiritual deadness. The sinner existed before, to be
sure, but he existed devoid of life. ". . . all things are become
new" (5:17). The new thing is life in Christ, with all that
entails.

John gives a word concerning this great miracle, explaining how it takes place: Christ "came unto his own, and his
own received him not" (John 1:11). He came unto His own
things, His rights as Messiah, but His own nation Israel received Him not. "But as many as received him, to them gave
he power [and the word *power* means *the right,* or *the authority*] to become the sons of God . . ." (v. 12). I am sure
there are few who have the name Pentecost, but the
children in our family have the right and the authority to
use that name. They were born into the family; they have
the right and authority to use that name by virtue of a
natural birth from two parents who were named Pentecost.
John actually says, "As many as received Him, to them gave
He *the authority* to become the sons of God." One became
a Jew because of his blood line: he was born of Jewish parents; he was born of blood. One was born naturally because
of the will of the flesh or because of the will of man. But
blood and flesh and the human will have nothing to do with

the salvation that is given to a man in Jesus Christ. It is the Holy Spirit who vivifies. When one hears the gospel, the way of salvation, preached, the Holy Spirit begins to nudge the hearer to Christ, in exactly the same way the eagle begins to nudge her fledglings into motion. As the movement of the eaglet is the result of the mother's nudging, so the receiving of Christ as saviour is the result of the spirit's nudging.

Recently I stayed in a home in an apartment building. It was quite evident, about two o'clock in the morning, that there was a new life right over my head. That new life was very, very hungry. I heard two feet hit the floor and go into what must have been the kitchen. I heard the refrigerator door open and slam. I heard some fumbling around the stove. All the time the new life was manifesting itself. Then those feet walked from the kitchen back into the room right over my head and soon there was a blissful silence. I didn't have to ask my host and hostess the next morning, "Is there a baby upstairs?" The manifestation of life was evident. So the result of the Spirit's work in regeneration is manifest by new life.

There was one who came to the Lord Jesus Christ who seemed to have everything that the human heart could desire. He had been elevated to a position of prominence in his own nation, and because of his abilities as an interpreter of the law he had been made a member of the supreme court of his people: he was a member of the Sanhedrin. With that position went all of the honor and respect and earthly glory and pomp that could be enjoyed by any individual. He wielded great power, not only in the spiritual realm, but in the political, economic, social and educational realms as well. Here is one who, because of his attainments and position and power, must have accumulated a great material fortune. Yet

he comes to the Lord Jesus Christ with a heart that is completely unsatisfied. His position, his power, his influence, his
responsibility, his material wealth could not satisfy because
he had no basic assurance of forgiveness of sins. He had no
assurance of the possession of eternal life, and no assurance
of an acceptance before God. He came by night to have a
personal interview with the One who had been speaking
about the way of righteousness and the way of access into the
Kingdom of God. We know this man as Nicodemus.

Even though it was early in our Lord's ministry, He had
attracted wide attention. There was a movement going on
in the nation Israel that had shaken it as few events in the
history of that nation had ever done. Some short time before,
there had appeared a rugged individualist who lifted up a
trumpet voice and summoned those who feared God. He had
appeared, not in the elect society of the temple, nor among
the rulers of the Jews. He had appeared in the desert. Even
though he was the son of a priest, he had not robed himself
with priestly vestments. He wore coarse camel's hair and
bound his outer garments together with simple leather
thongs. No carefully embroidered girdle was his. He had
come, not with a message to pacify and satisfy the hearts of
the people of Israel; but with a denunciatory message that
had caused them to be convicted of their sin. Even though
they did not agree with his announcements of impending
judgment, they had not been able to refrain from going out
to hear him preach. John the Baptist had literally taken the
nation by storm. Throughout the length and breadth of the
land of Palestine people were made conscious of their own
sinfulness; they were made conscious of a Holy God, who
must judge them; they were made conscious of their own
need of cleansing. And so, those who came to John to confess

their sins were baptized by him with a view to forgiveness. John did not claim to dispense forgiveness, but he did introduce Messiah, "the Lamb of God, which taketh away the sin of the world" (John 1:29). John was bringing before their minds the whole line of teaching in the Old Testament that there would be no complete and permanent forgiveness of sins until the Messiah, the sin-bearer, should come. The people came to John and listened to him condemn them for their iniquity and unrighteousness and heard him herald the Lamb of God, and say, "Repent ye: for the kingdom of heaven is at hand . . ." (Matthew 3:2). Because they had been taught the Old Testament Scriptures, they would know that when Messiah comes and institutes His kingdom, one of the first things that Messiah will do will be to grant them forgiveness of sin. And so, those who were convicted, those who confessed their need, came to John to identify themselves with this believing group who were preparing themselves through John's baptism to meet the Messiah.

When Jesus Christ came, drawing John's followers to Himself, the Lord made the same announcement that John had made: "the kingdom of heaven is at hand" (Matthew 4:17). He presented Himself as the Lamb of God who will take away the sin of the world: He also presented Himself as the Messiah. He was the Saviour and the Sovereign, the Redeemer who would also reign. Immediately the people wanted to know the authority by which the Lord Jesus Christ came. Did He have the right to claim to be Messiah? Did He have the authority from God that would enable Him to forgive sins?

After the Lord had gone into the temple and had driven out those who were buying and selling, He possessed God's temple as Messiah. He worked a number of miracles and signs to prove that He had the right to come as Messiah and to possess the Temple in God's name. He had the power that would enable Him to grant forgiveness of sin.

When the leaders of the nation Israel heard that Messiah had come and that there was One within their midst who was working miracles, they were interested. As the supreme court, it was the responsibility of the Sanhedrin to make pronouncements in all religious matters. If Messiah had come, it would be up to the Sanhedrin to inform the people in Israel that He was there. On the other hand, if He were a false messiah, and there were many false messiahs, it would be the responsibility of this Court to evaluate Him, to make a public pronouncement that it gave no credence to His message. Evidently Nicodemus, either as the official representative of the Sanhedrin, or on his own initiative, made his way to Christ to get His answers concerning the forgiveness of sin, how a man comes into Messiah's kingdom, how a man can be right with God. Nicodemus addressed Him as "Rabbi," that is, a teacher. But He is no ordinary teacher for He does not have the authority of the theological school of Hillel or the theological school of Shammai behind Him. Nicodemus recognized Jesus as "a teacher *come from God* . . ." (John 3:2); not come from men, nor from the Sanhedrin, but come from God. As a teacher come from God He is to be believed and trusted; He will have an authoritative message as to how a man may be made righteous. John the Baptist had come with a one-sided message. He pointed to the leaders and said, "You generation of vipers!" or "You snakes in the grass!" and condemned them for their iniquity. It was a preaching of judgment with no message as to how to escape that judgment apart from the Lamb of God. The nation Israel was quivering before a righteous God for they knew that God must judge them for their sins, but the way of escape had not been provided. And here, with his own heart burdened, and with his own need laid bare, Nicodemus comes to Christ and acknowledges that Christ has come with a message from God.

Our Lord went to the root of the problem with His declaration, "Except a man be born again, he cannot see the kingdom of God" (v. 3). The Judaism of our Lord's day taught that if one had had the good fortune to be born of Jewish parents, his salvation was assured, for Abraham would sit at the gate of hell and would prevent any descendant of Abraham from passing through its gates. What was necessary in addition to that physical birth could be supplied by their own works, by fulfilling the law, by observing the feast days, by offering sacrifices, by paying tithes into the temple treasury. Yet our Lord answered Nicodemus and gave His declaration that unless a man be born again he cannot see the Kingdom of God. Entrance into Messiah's Kingdom, establishment of a relationship with God, the forgiveness of sins, the gift of eternal life did not come because one was born a physical descendant of Abraham, or because he kept the law, offered sacrifices and paid tithes. Salvation depends upon a new birth, and this declaration has not changed over the two thousand years since our Lord spoke these words.

Nicodemus replied to our Lord's declaration with a question. It was a natural question because our Lord was speaking to him of a mystery that the Old Testament had not revealed. Nicodemus asked, "How can a man be born when he is old? Can he enter a second time into his mother's womb and be born?" When Christ mentioned a birth, Nicodemus thought of natural generation. When he heard of a second

birth, he concluded that the second birth is only a duplica-
tion of the first natural birth. And, of course, a physical re-
birth is impossible.

The Lord Jesus proceeded to explain the work of the Spirit
in the new birth. He said, "Verily, verily, I say unto thee,
Except a man be born of water and of the Spirit, he cannot
enter into the kingdom of God" (v. 5). This is a well-known
but much debated verse because of the depth of its meaning.
It is difficult to understand all that our Lord had to reveal to
this learned doctor of the Old Testament. If you have won-
dered at all the ramifications, be consoled that Nicodemus,
who knew so much about the Old Testament, didn't understand it either. It had to be explained and re-explained to
him. Our Lord said, "Except a man be born of water and
breath, he cannot enter into the kingdom of God." He uses
the figures of water and breath. We have to understand these
two symbols to get our Lord's teaching in this passage.

Water is used as a figure in different ways. It is sometimes
used as a symbol of the new birth or regeneration, and it is
also used as a symbol of washing or of cleansing. It has been
used as a symbol of the Word of God. Our problem lies in
determining which of these meanings was in our Lord's mind
when He employed the word in this passage. Water, in reference to the Word of God, is well known. Jesus said, "Now ye
are clean through the word which I have spoken unto you"
(John 15:3). Peter writes, "Seeing ye have purified your souls
in obeying the truth through the Spirit unto unfeigned love
of the brethren, see that ye love one another with a pure heart
fervently: Being born again, not of corruptible seed, but of
incorruptible, by the word of God, which liveth and abideth
for ever" (I Peter 1:22-23). Peter teaches us that this miracle
of the new birth is accomplished through the instrumentality

of the Word of God, and the Word of God is a means of cleansing the believer who has fallen into sin.

This thought was in our Lord's mind when He took the disciples into the upper room, poured water into a basin, girded Himself with a towel and proceeded to wash the disciples' feet. He said, "He that is washed needeth not save to wash his feet . . ." (John 13:10). Literally, Jesus said, "He that is completely bathed all over, needs not except to sponge his feet." The water here is related to cleansing, that which will make one acceptable to God. When our Lord said, "Except a man be born of water . . ." it may be that He was emphasizing the truth that the Word of God is the instrument that will be used by God to convict of sin, to show our need of a Saviour, and to reveal to us the Lamb of God that taketh away the sin of the world. In that sense, the Word of God will do today what John the Baptist did when he stood in the wilderness and looked at those people and said, "You generation of vipers!" The Word of God convicts, reproves, enlightens, exhorts, reveals, not only our need but the Lord Jesus Christ who can meet that need. And if we understand the verse in that sense, the instrument that convicts is not the agent that produces the new birth. The instrument that convicts is the Word of God, but it is the Spirit who produces the new birth. The Word of God, energized by the Spirit of God, produces the new birth. If the Word of God is preached, but is not energized, in both its utterance and its hearing, by the Spirit of God, it would be as though the poetry of Shakespeare were spoken. It would produce no result. The Word of God must be energized by the Spirit of God in order to produce its work.

Paul says, "Not by works of righteousness which we have done, but according to his mercy he saved us . . ." (Titus 3:5).

The Apostle, was doing the same thing our Lord did with Nicodemus. Nicodemus had in his mind the question, "Will John's baptism save us, will keeping the law save us, will observance of the feast and the rituals of Israel save us?" The Lord had to say, "No. It is not by works of righteousness which you do, but by the water and by the spirit." Paul, too, refers to the water and the Spirit. When he wrote, "by the washing of regeneration, and renewing of the Holy Ghost" (v. 5), he was not speaking of two things, but of one. Salvation is a washing and a re-creating. That is why Paul refers to believers in II Corinthians as a "new creation," or a "new creature." The water of John 3:5 is the washing of regeneration and the Spirit of John 3:5 is the renewing by the Holy Ghost. Such would be an acceptable interpretation.

However, water was used in the Old Testament, but not primarily in reference to the Word. What we have said concerning the interpretation of water and Spirit, we have done by looking into the Epistles, by looking ahead from the standpoint of Jesus and Nicodemus. But what did Nicodemus know about what would be written later? Not a thing. Therefore, instead of looking ahead into the Epistles for our interpretation, we have to look back into the context in which Nicodemus was brought up. When you look backward, instead of forward, in the Word of God, water always meant one thing: cleansing. In the Old Testament ritual, water was the emblem of cleansing. When an article was unclean and it was purchased for temple use and was to be set apart to God, it was either plunged into water, or water was poured over it, or water was sprinkled upon it. By the application of water it became ceremonially clean. When an object or a person was defiled, it was made ceremonially clean by the application of the water of purification. Thus, to the Jews, steeped in the

Old Testament, water meant cleansing. That would be the first thing that would have come into Nicodemus' mind when our Lord said, "Except a man be born of water . . ." Nicodemus would say, "Yes, except a man be cleansed, he cannot see the Kingdom of God. But the problem is, How does one get cleansed?" Remember, Nicodemus had been out observing John in his ministry, and he saw John administer water of cleansing. He wanted to know if John's cleansing was sufficient. If the Jews submitted to John's baptism, would they receive the cleansing that is necessary to bring them into the Kingdom of God? The Lord said that John's baptism was not enough, for a man must be born not only of water, but of breath, or by interpretation, by the Spirit of God. John's baptism had its place in reference to the nation Israel because John was singling out a people who believed that they were sinners; he was identifying a people who claimed to need a Messiah; he was identifying a group who were trusting God to send a Saviour; but that baptism couldn't save them. There had to be, in addition, the work of the Spirit of God. A priest might provide water for cleansing but only God could provide the Spirit of God which could effect the new birth. So to this the Lord said that a man must be born again. The explanation was that this new birth must be one that cleanses and gives new life by the power of the Spirit of God.

Our Lord explained this truth to the learned doctor of the law who was so ignorant of spiritual things and the facts of the new birth. First, our Lord points out that the truth He has been teaching is not subject to human understanding or human comprehension. Christ was emphasizing that the new birth is the work of God. Here is a mystery which a man can understand in the Spiritual realm only as well as a child understands the facts of his own advent into this world.

A child recognizes that he is here, but he knows not from whence he came. So it is of one who is born by the Spirit of God.

Then, our Lord points out that this is a matter of divine revelation for He says, "no man hath ascended up to heaven, but he that came down from heaven, even the Son of man which is in heaven" (John 3:13). Because He was in heaven and has come from heaven, He can make a revelation about the things of heaven; He can make a revelation concerning the way of entrance into heaven.

Christ also points out that this new birth is received by faith. He goes back into the Old Testament to that familiar story where the children of Israel, because of their constant griping and murmuring, were smitten by the scourge of poisonous serpents, and multitudes in Israel died. Moses went to God to find some way by which this judgment might be relieved. He was told to take some brass or bronze and to fashion it into the likeness of a serpent, and raise it up on a pole in the center of the camp. God then announced through Moses that any individual who looked on that serpent would be healed. That was to be an act of faith. They had to turn their eyes on the likeness of that which had brought judgment to them. And when they looked, they were healed by faith.

As you had absolutely nothing to do with your own human conception, prenatal development and physical birth, you have nothing to do with your spiritual birth. As you were born into this world through the act of others, so you are born into the family of God by the action of Another. Only the Spirit of God can give life to that which was dead; can take that one who was without life and re-create him so that he becomes a son of God. That which is born of the flesh will always partake of the nature of its progenitors, and that which is born of the Spirit partakes of the nature of its progenitor. Salvation is the work of God who, through the Word of God, accomplishes a cleansing and grants new life by the work of the Spirit. If you accept Jesus Christ as your own personal Saviour, you may have the gift of salvation.

10

THE BAPTIZING MINISTRY
OF THE SPIRIT

"FOR BY ONE SPIRIT ARE WE ALL BAPTIZED INTO ONE BODY, whether we be Jews or Gentiles, whether we be bond or free; and have been all made to drink into one Spirit" (I Corinthians 12:13). There are few, if any, of the great doctrines concerning the person and work of the Holy Spirit about which there is as much confusion and misunderstanding as the doctrine of the baptism of the Holy Spirit. A great many different interpretations have been presented to explain what is involved in this baptizing work. Many well-meaning but misguided children of God are seeking some second work of grace, or some special blessing that God has reserved for a chosen few, calling it the baptism of the Spirit. Relegating it to the realm of experience, they conscientiously wait before God, asking God to give them this great experience.

As we look at the basic text for our study, I Corinthians 12:13, we want to emphasize four facts. First, baptism is the unique experience for believers in this age; second, it is the universal experience of all believers in this age; third, the baptism of the Holy Spirit unites believers to the body of Christ, and fourth, the baptizing work of the Holy Spirit unites us to Christ Himself.

The Apostle Paul tells us that the baptism of the Spirit is "by one Spirit," and he is revealing that this is a unique experience in this present age of grace in which we live. It is not an experience which was the privilege of the saints who lived in the Old Testament time, or who lived before the death and resurrection of Christ, or who lived before the advent of the Holy Spirit into the world on the day of Pentecost. When the Lord spoke of the Holy Spirit in John 14:16, He spoke of the coming of the Holy Spirit as a future event. While the Holy Spirit came on certain individuals in the Old Testament, He had not come to take up residence in all believers. Our Lord spoke prophetically in John 14:16: "And I will pray the Father, and he *shall* give you another Comforter. . . ." Also, "But the Comforter, which is the Holy Ghost, whom the Father *will* send in my name, he *shall* teach you all things" (v. 26). Again, the future tense is emphasized. The Holy Spirit could not perform his baptizing ministry until Jesus Christ had been crucified; until He had been glorified at the right hand of the Father; and until He had asked the Father to send the Spirit to indwell believers. Christ said, "Howbeit when he, the Spirit of truth, is come, he will guide you into all truth: for he shall not speak of himself; . . . and he will shew you things to come" (John 16:13). Once again we observe that the Lord was speaking a prophecy. As He stood on the last day of the feast, He cried, "If any man thirst, let him come unto me, and drink. He that believeth on me, as the scripture hath said, out of his belly *shall* flow rivers of living water . . ." (John 7:37).

Our Lord again speaks prophetically as He says, "John truly baptized with water; but *ye shall be* baptized with the Holy Ghost *not many days hence* . . ." (Acts 1:5). At the time of His ascension, Jesus gave a promise to the disciples that they would receive this unique experience of the baptism of the Holy Spirit shortly. When you read later in the Book of Acts, and in Galatians, Colossians and Corinthians, concerning the baptism of the Spirit, it is always spoken of as something that has already taken place. We can only conclude that the baptizing work of the Spirit took place some time between the ascension of Christ and the time that the apostles wrote that believers have already been baptized.

The baptizing work of the Holy Spirit is the universal experience of all believers in this age. In his First Letter to the Corinthians, the Apostle Paul was writing to the sorriest congregation of believers that are described in the Word of God. This little assembly was divided over personalities, comparing preacher with preacher. They were divided over doctrines, some holding to the truths of the Word of God, and some holding to false doctrines. There were false practices. There was misuse of the Lord's table. Paul had to set them right in respect to doctrinal, practical and moral defects. Yet he says to that whole assembly, "You have *all* been baptized. Not only you spiritual ones; not only you sanctified ones; but you have *all* been baptized by the Spirit." This shows very clearly that this work of the Holy Spirit in baptism is not related to a believer's experience, his growth, his knowledge, his Godliness or sanctification; otherwise, it could not be the experience of all believers.

In his Letter to the Galatians, the Apostle says, ". . . ye are all the children of God by faith in Christ Jesus" (3:26). The first great fact that Paul has put before us is that faith in the Lord Jesus Christ makes one a child of God. Paul was writing to believers, not to a mixed multitude of believers and unbelievers. What does he say about these believers? ". . . as many of you as have been baptized into Christ have put on Christ" (v. 27). He is teaching that those who, by faith in Christ Jesus, are the children of God have been baptized into the body of Christ. They have been baptized into Christ and have put on Christ. "There is neither Jew nor Greek, . . . bond nor free, . . . neither male nor female: for ye are all one in Christ Jesus" (v. 28). This experience of the baptism of the Holy Spirit is the universal experience of every one who has accepted Jesus Christ as a personal Saviour. One is regenerated, baptized by the Holy Spirit, indwelt and sealed by the Spirit, all in the same moment of time. Chronologically, there is no separation.

In the Word of God no individual is ever exhorted to be baptized with the Holy Spirit. If this baptism were a second work of grace; if it were something to be experienced sometime subsequent to salvation, the Apostle certainly would have laid down the basis on which we are to receive the baptism. He would have given us commandments concerning our responsibility to get this baptism, and we would have exhortations to "Be baptized with the Spirit." However, no believer, under any circumstances, is ever invited to seek the baptism of the Holy Spirit. Therefore, it shows us that this is a universal experience for all believers. We need not seek it, pray for it, or try to get it. It is something that God has already given to us by faith in the Lord Jesus Christ.

"By one Spirit are we all baptized *into one body* . . ." (I Corinthians 12:13). By this, the Apostle teaches us that the baptism by the Spirit unites believers to the body of Jesus Christ. To understand this teaching, we have to be clear on the New Testament teaching concerning the church. What is the church? Two different figures are used to teach the relationship of believer with believer in the church. Believers are, first of all, called a temple. As members of a temple, we are pictured as stones in a building. The Apostle Paul pictures the Lord Jesus Christ as a foundation (I Corinthians 3).

He pictures the Apostles as masons who are putting stones into the building, and he exhorts those spiritual masons to be careful what kind of stones they use, because every man's work shall be tried. The Apostle Peter also uses the figure of a building as he tells us that we, as living stones, are members of this building (I Peter 2:5). Now, when we think of stones in a building, we think of something inanimate. Nobody ever saw a brick get up and walk. You may have seen a brick fly but somebody had to make it fly. But while Scripture does speak of believers as being stones in a building, and living stones at that, the second figure employed concerning the church brings to our minds the concept of life. The believers in the Lord Jesus Christ, or the church, are pictured as a body! "Know ye not that your bodies are the members of Christ?" (I Corinthians 6:15). Or again, Paul says, "as the body is one, and hath many members, and all the members of that one body, being many, are one body: so also is Christ" (I Corinthians 12:12). In this figure, believers are pictured as members of a body. The Apostle says that some members are in the body as hands; some are in the body as feet; some are eyes; some are ears. As each member of the physical body has a different function to perform, so each member in the body of Christ has a different function to perform. In this figure of the church as the body, we find something else which ought to be emphasized. The physical body needs a head as a directing and coördinating agent. Christ is that head of the church: God "hath put all things under his feet, and gave him to be the *head* over all things to the church, Which is his body, the fulness of him that filleth all in all" (Ephesians 1:22). The Apostle shows us that as there is a relationship between the head and the body, so there is between Christ and the church. Just as the body would be lifeless without being joined to the head, and the head would be incomplete without a body through which the head could function, so the church is the body, the fullness, or that which completes the One who is all in all.

The Apostle repeats the fact that Christ is the head of the body: ". . . the husband is the head of the wife, even as Christ is the head of the church: and he is the saviour of the body" (Ephesians 5:23). In this figure of the body, it is quite evident that the life that is in one part of the body is in every part of the body. There is not one kind of life in the hand, and a different life in the ear, and another life in the eye. The body has one life principle, and that principle is in every cell of this natural body. The Apostle teaches us, in I Corinthians 12:13, that the baptizing work of the Holy Spirit is that work of the Spirit that takes us, at the moment of our salvation, and joins us as a living member of the body of Jesus Christ. You were born into the family of God, but you were not born into the body of Christ. You were born into the family, but you became a member of the body of Christ by being baptized into that body, or joined to that body, by the work of the Holy Spirit of God.

In his Letter to the Ephesians, Paul speaks of the unity of the body, and he says that we are to endeavor to keep the unity of the Spirit in the bond of peace. Each member of the body is to be at peace, or in harmony, with every other member of the body. He mentions the things that unite the body into a unit: one Spirit, one call, one Lord, one faith, one baptism, and one God and Father of all, who is above all and through all and in you all. Now, what is the one baptism? It cannot be outward, water baptism, which has done more to divide believers than any other one teaching of the Word of God. What is it that unites believers one to the other? It is the work of the Holy Spirit uniting them, or baptizing them, into the one body.

Observe that when a believer is joined to the body of Christ, he does not lose his individual identity. If you were to build a building out of poured concrete, there would be a unity in that building but everything that went into that building would have lost its separate identity in the whole. That is not true of our relationship in the body. When we, by the Spirit of God, are joined as living members, we maintain our own separate identity. There is a oneness of life: the same life that is in me as a believer in the Lord Jesus Christ is in you as a believer in the Lord Jesus Christ. The reason we can fulfill the commandment of Christ to love one another is that when we love one another we are loving that of which we are a part. This love ought to be the most natural thing because the same life is in you that is in me. The baptism of the Spirit unites believers one to another in the body of Christ.

The baptizing work of the Holy Spirit not only unites us one with another in the body in which Christ is head, but it unites us to Christ Himself: "For as many of you as have been baptized *into Christ* have put on Christ" (Galatians 3:27). We have been baptized into Christ, as Christ explained to the disciples: "At that day ye shall know that I am in my Father, and ye in me, and I in you (John 14:20). The same oneness that existed between the Father and the Son was to exist between the Son and believers. How was that relationship to be instituted? By the baptizing work of the Holy Spirit. When the Spirit came on the day of Pentecost and baptized those who had accepted Jesus Christ as Lord and Saviour into the body of Christ, they were baptized into Christ Jesus Himself. A oneness exists not only between believer and believer because the life of God resided in each believer, but between the believer and the Son of God because the life in the child of God is identical with the life of the Son of God. Perhaps the most characteristic word in the theology of the Apostle Paul is that one phrase, "*in* Christ." In Ephesians 1:3 he says, "Blessed be the God and Father of our Lord Jesus Christ, who hath blessed us with all spiritual blessings in heavenly places *in* Christ." The Apostle is emphasizing that every spiritual blessing that an infinite God could devise to give to the children of God has been given to them *in Christ Jesus.* We have been lifted out of our position in the world, out of our relationship to the god of this world, Satan; we have been put into a new relationship *in* Christ Jesus. And how did those privileges become ours? Because the Spirit of God baptized us into Christ Jesus.

Many of God's children feel that the baptizing work of the Holy Spirit is synonomous with the filling of the Spirit. The filling of the Spirit has to do with our Christian walk, day by day. It has to do with divine empowerment, so that a believer may live, under the control of the Holy Spirit of God, a life that is pleasing to God. Those who equate the baptizing work and the filling work are asking God for a baptism of power. On the authority of the Word of God, baptism has to do, not with our daily experience or our daily walk, but with our position, our relationship to God. By one Spirit, in a special way in this age, all believers have been baptized into one body so that we sustain a new relationship, one to the other, and to Christ.

11

THE SEALING MINISTRY
OF THE SPIRIT

INFINITE WISDOM CANNOT DEVISE MORE BLESSINGS FOR THE children of God than have already been provided in the Lord Jesus Christ. In the first chapter of Ephesians the Apostle enumerates some of the spiritual blessings that are ours. He states that we were chosen in Christ before the foundation of the world; we were made Holy and without blame before Him in love (v. 4). We have been predestinated and have been adopted in Jesus Christ (v. 5). We have been given redemption and the forgiveness of sin (v. 7). We have been enlightened in that God abounded toward us in all wisdom and prudence (v. 8). We have received the revelation of the deep things of God for He has made known unto us the mystery of His will (v. 9). We have been given an inheritance in Christ Jesus, according to His own purpose (v. 11). Coming to the climax of the blessings that are ours, the Apostle says, ". . . after that ye believed, ye were sealed with that holy Spirt of promise" (v. 13).

On at least three occasions in the New Testament, reference is made to the sealing ministry of the Holy Spirit. This very significant word *seal* has lost a great deal of its import to us today because we no longer use it in ordinary commerce as it was used in Paul's day. Yet it is a word that is fraught with both doctrinal and practical significance that ought to cause our hearts to rejoice and give us a quiet assurance before God as we see what God does for us in sealing us with that Holy Spirit of promise.

"All the promises of God in him are yea, and in him Amen, unto the glory of God by us. Now he which stablisheth us with you in Christ, and hath anointed us, is God; Who hath also sealed us, and given the earnest of the Spirit in our hearts" (II Corinthians 1:20-22). Paul says it is God who hath sealed us, and the Holy Spirit is the One with whom we are sealed. This then is as much a part of His work in salvation as His work of giving His Son over to the death of the cross, or His work of calling us out of darkness into His marvelous light, or His work in forgiving us of our sins and imputing the righteousness of Christ to us. This then is but one factor in the total saving work of God the Father as He would translate us out of the kingdom of darkness into the Kingdom of the Son of His love. God has sealed us and has given us, as a gracious gift, the earnest of the Spirit in our hearts.

This seal is placed in our hearts. God reaches down to the inner recesses of man, an area where no man himself can penetrate, in order to place an identifying sign. If a mark is put upon the heart of man, it has to be put there by One who searches and knows the heart; One who can penetrate to the depths of the heart. This again emphasizes that this seal-ing work must be the work of God for it is not an external identifying sign, but rather an internal identification.

The sealing with the Holy Spirit of promise is based upon personal faith in the Lord Jesus Christ as a Saviour. This sealing takes place the very moment that one accepts Jesus Christ as his own Saviour (Ephesians 1:13). The Apostle literally writes, "In whom ye also trusted, after that ye heard the word of truth, the gospel of your salvation: in whom also *having believed,* ye were sealed." I have translated that passage literally for the apostle did not say "after that ye believed," as in the King James translation, as though at some subsequent time God does something for you which He didn't do the moment you believed. The Apostle emphasizes here that that sealing takes place at the time of believing. "Because ye believe," or, "when ye believe," ye, at that moment, on the basis of faith, were sealed with that Holy Spirit of promise. The sealing, then, does not depend upon an individual purging himself, or coming to some position of sanctification, so that he is eligible to receive this identifying mark from God. It is the work of God that is based solely upon faith in the Lord Jesus Christ.

In Ephesians 4:30, we see that this sealing with the Holy Spirit must be universal among all believers in Jesus Christ: "And grieve not the holy Spirit of God, whereby ye are sealed unto the day of redemption." The Apostle was writing to all the Ephesian believers, and he said all these believers had the potentiality to grieve the Holy Spirit. If the possibility is there that they can grieve Him, they must have been sealed by the Holy Spirit, and sealed unto the day of redemption. The Apostle has told us (Ephesians 2:22) that, as believers, they were builded together for an habitation of God through the Spirit. God the Holy Spirit had taken up residence within them and it is because of this universal indwelling of the Holy Spirit in every blood-bought believer that they could grieve the Holy Spirit. We observe from this passage that being sealed with the Holy Spirit is a universal experience for every child of God.

What does it mean to us, practically, to be sealed with the Holy Spirit? Let us consider some illustrations from the Word of God where the seal is used as a figure. First of all, we have the story of Daniel in the lion's den: "the king commanded, and they brought Daniel, and cast him into the den of lions. Now the king spake and said unto Daniel, Thy God whom thou servest continually, he will deliver thee. And a stone was brought, and laid upon the mouth of the den; and the king sealed it with his own signet, and with the signet of his lords; that the purpose might not be changed concerning Daniel" (Daniel 6:16-17). Here we find seal used as a sign of security. Daniel was secured in the lion's den and there was no escape from his confinement therein. In a day when so few people could write, a man had a signet engraved as his own identifying mark. He wore it on a chain about his waist or, perchance, on a ring about his finger. He guarded it very carefully because if one used that signet, even without his consent, it was as valid as though the man used it himself. When the king commanded that Daniel be confined and then gave his signet to be affixed to the seal on that lion's den, it meant that only one who had greater power than the king had the right to break that seal.

You may remember a similar incident in the gospel records. When the Pharisees remembered that Jesus Christ had promised that He would rise from the dead, they went to the Roman authorities and asked them to make the tomb secure, because they were afraid Christ's body might be stolen and that a false report of His resurrection would go abroad. So what did the Roman authorities do? They affixed a Roman seal to that tomb. Now, the seal had no strength in itself, but it had authority and could confine what was within because of the authority of the one who imposed the seal. It was the authority of the one affixing the seal that gave the seal its power to secure. The Apostle Paul says (Ephesians

4:30) that we have been sealed, and that we are sealed unto the day of redemption. God the Father is the sealer and The Holy Spirit is the seal. Thus the Spirit is the mark of our absolute security; the mark given to us to assure us that we shall arrive at God's ordained destination for us. What is it that keeps us, as God's children, safe? It is not our own strength or power; it is not our own righteousness or works; it is not what we do for God after we are saved and have accepted Christ as Saviour. We are secured because God the Father has given to us God the Holy Spirit as our seal. If one could rise up with greater power than the One who sealed us, greater power than the power of God, that one might break the seal, and then we who have been made secure to the extent of God's power could then become insecure. But because our God is an omnipotent God and none can claim authority over Him, our security rests in the hand of the One who has secured us for Himself. If we were dealing with the doctrine of security, we could give any number of reasons, from the Word of God, why we believe that the one who accepts Jesus Christ as a personal Saviour has a finished and completed salvation. Were there no other than that of sealing, it would be sufficient, for as Daniel could be sealed and secured within the lion's den and as the body of the Lord Jesus Christ could be secured within that tomb by the seal imposed by a king or government, we are secured in the Lord Jesus Christ with the Holy Spirit.

Our Lord, speaking of the flock over which He is Shepherd, says, "I am the good shepherd, and know my sheep . . ." (John 10:14). Again, He says, "My sheep hear my voice, and I know them . . ." (v. 27). On what does Christ's knowledge of His sheep depend? You may say, "It depends upon His omniscience, and that is sufficient for me." An omniscient God could

never forget one of His sheep. But there is something more
than His omniscience that causes Him to know His sheep.
God has an identifying mark that He Himself sees in the
heart of each one of His own. He recognizes His own Spirit
which He has placed within us as the seal that we are His
forever.

In the Old Testament we are brought face to face with the
wicked King Ahab who coveted a neighbor's vineyard. All
the material things that Ahab had could not satisfy him, and
he looked for more material possessions to add to what he had.
"Jezebel his wife said unto him, Dost thou now govern the
kingdom of Israel? arise, and eat bread, and let thine heart be
merry: I will give thee the vineyard of Naboth the Jezreelite.
So she wrote letters in Ahab's name, and sealed them with his
seal, and sent the letters unto the elders and to the nobles
that were in his city, dwelling with Naboth. And she wrote
in the letters, saying, Proclaim a fast, and set Naboth on high
among the people" (I Kings 21:7-9). Through her deceptions,
Jezebel acquired for Ahab that to which he had no right
according to Levitical laws of inheritance. Notice how she
did it. She wrote letters and then made them official by sealing
them with Ahab's seal. This seal was a mark of authenticity.
Even though the whole letter was a forgery, it looked like the
king's letter because it had his seal affixed to it.

When we come to the New Testament we are reminded of
the word in John 1:12: "as many as received him, to them
gave he power [authority, or right] to become the sons of
God. . . ." On what basis? God the Father has taken us, who
have no right to His name, and by sealing us with the Holy
Spirit has authenticated us, who were sons of the evil one,
as the sons of God. And when God has authenticated us as
His own, who can debate the authentic mark that God Him-

self has put upon us? When we affirm that we are the children
of God we are not imposters; we are not those who have no
right to His name. We have every right because God has
authenticated us with the seal of the Holy Spirit.

The prophet Jeremiah did a very strange thing. He had
been telling the people for a long time that all the Jews were
going to be carried out of the land of Palestine and that Jerusalem was about to be destroyed and overrun by enemies.
That means that property values in Jerusalem were dropping
all the time. Who would want to buy a piece of property in
a place that would soon be a rubble heap? But God had also
told Jeremiah that the people would not only be scattered;
they would be brought back together into their land again.
God told Jeremiah to go out and buy up a piece of property.
The natural question would be, "What for, Lord? I'm no
young man, and the people are going to be out of here for
seventy years, and what good will it do?" But the Lord revealed that some day some of Jeremiah's descendants would
be glad he bought this property. He was instructed to buy it,
take the title deed to it and put it in a safe place where it
could be found again. Jeremiah says, "And I subscribed the
evidence, and sealed it, and took witnesses, and weighed him
the money in the balances. So I took the evidence of the purchase, both that which was sealed according to the law and
custom, and that which was open: And I gave the evidence of
the purchase unto Baruch . . ." (Jeremiah 32:10-12). "Thus
saith the Lord of hosts, the God of Israel; Take these evidences,
this evidence of the purchase, both which is sealed, and this
evidence which is open; and put them in an earthen vessel, that
they may continue many days. For thus saith the Lord of
hosts, the God of Israel; Houses and fields and vineyards shall
be possessed again in this land . . ." (vv. 14-15). The title deed

to the land, which Jeremiah had sealed according to the law, was the mark of ownership, of possession. The seal signified a finished transaction. If one were to question Jeremiah's right to that land, or the right of Jeremiah's descendants, the copy that had been sealed would settle the right. If all Jerusalem were destroyed and all the records were lost, the sealed copy that was put away in the earthen jar would certify ownership.

They have been branding cattle in Texas for a good many years but they are still trying to find a foolproof brand, or a foolproof method of marking cattle. Why? Because nobody has yet devised a brand that somebody can't alter if he wants to superimpose his mark over the rightful mark of ownership. When God would identify His own and signify a completed transaction, He does not put the seal where the devil can alter God's identifying mark into a forgery that will deliver God's child into the hand of Satan. When Satan's great masterpiece comes on the world scene during the tribulation period, and he institutes the great politico-religious system of which he is the head, one of the first things he establishes is the mark of the beast. What is the mark of the beast? It is simply an identifying mark, a brand, if you please, or a seal. And Satan, in imitation of what God does, imposes his seal on his subjects. But he has to do it on the forehead, or on the palm of the hand, of the one who submits to his authority. Satan can't go into the heart to take out the identifying mark of God, nor can he superimpose an internal mark. God's identifying mark is a public sign to any adversary: *"No trespassing— hands off! This is My property!"*

In the Book of Esther we find that when Haman conspired against Mordecai to put the Jews to death, he addressed a petition to Ahasuerus, and said, "If it please the king, let it be written that they may be destroyed: and I will pay ten thousand talents of silver to the hands of those that have the charge of the business, to bring it into the king's treasuries. And the king took his ring from his hand, and gave it unto Haman . . ." (3:9-10). Again, we read, "Behold, I have given Esther the house of Haman, and him they have hanged upon the gallows, because he laid his hand upon the Jews. Write ye also for the Jews, as it liketh you, in the king's name, and seal it with the king's ring: for the writing which is written in the king's name, and sealed with the king's ring, may no man reverse . . ." (8:7-8). In these two passages we find that the ruling monarch made an appointment; he gave a man authority; he conferred privileges and responsibilities upon him, and the sign of authority was the signet or the seal from the king which he had the right to use. The appointee was not operating in his own name, he had no authority of himself; but he was operating under delegated authority.

Christ said, ". . . in that day ye shall ask me nothing. Verily, verily, I say unto you, Whatsoever ye shall ask the Father in my name, he will give it you . . ." (John 16:23). We have rights before the Father. Did you ever realize that prayer is the exercise of authority? God said, ". . . concerning the work of my hands command ye me . . ." (Isaiah 45:11). By what authority do we tell God what to do? Not on our own authority, but by a delegated authority. The seal has been given to us. God the Holy Spirit is the One who confers upon us the right and authority so that in Christ's name we may come before the Father to present our petitions. When we approach the throne of grace it is not in our own merit or right, but in the name of the Lord Jesus Christ. By giving to us the seal of the Spirit, God has given to us the rights, privileges, authority and responsibility that belong to the child of God.

If you were to send a registered letter, that letter would be sealed in a pouch, and as that pouch passed from hand to hand, from train to train, each one whose hands touched that pouch would have to sign for it because sealing that bag was the guarantee given by our postal department that that letter would be delivered at its destination. And when God the Father has sealed us with the Holy Spirit it is the guarantee that we belong to Him. We are not spurious sons, but genuine sons. We are His personal possession and He guarantees that we will be delivered to our destination.

12

THE FILLING OF THE SPIRIT

OF ALL THE DOCTRINES IN THE REALM OF THE PERSON AND WORK of the Holy Spirit, there is none more important, as it relates to the believer's Christian life, than that of *the filling of the Spirit*. The Apostle Paul gives us a command: ". . . be not drunk with wine, wherein is excess; but be filled with the Spirit" (Ephesians 5:18). The Word of God divides men into several different classifications. After Paul has spoken of the natural man, he divides believers into two classifications: the carnal man, and the spiritual man (I Corinthians 2:9—3:4). The carnal man is the man who lives by the power of the flesh, according to the dictates of the flesh, and the spiritual man is the man who lives by the power of the Spirit. Those who walk worthily of the Lord are those who walk by the Spirit's power (Colossians 1:10), and those who walk after the manner of men are those who walk according to the flesh (I Corinthians 3:3). Paul says that if we walk by the Spirit we will not fulfill the lust of the flesh (Galatians 5:16). There the apostle is again dividing men into two classifications: those whose power in daily life is the Holy Spirit of God, and those whose strength is in the flesh. In each one of these categories men are divided on the basis of the filling with the Holy Spirit.

In Ephesians 5:18, Paul was dealing in the realm of the practical experience. He cannot be dealing in the realm of the positional; he cannot be relating this filling to a divine work of God which takes place the moment one accepts Jesus

Christ as a personal Saviour. If this were a positional work accomplished by the Holy Spirit at the moment of salvation, no command would be given to believers to be filled with the Spirit. If you examine the doctrine of the indwelling ministry of the Holy Spirit, never is a command given that we should be indwelt. When we consider the sealing ministry of the Holy Spirit, a command is never given that believers should be sealed. If we consider the baptizing work of the Holy Spirit, never in the Word of God can you find a command that the believer should seek the baptism of the Holy Spirit. As we, in previous studies, have traced these great doctrines in the area of the Spirit's ministries we have seen that they are related to our position in Christ and to that which God does for the child of God the moment he believes. But we move into an entirely different area, the area of practical experience, when the Apostle gives the command, "be filled with the Spirit."

Paul says, "be filled," and in the original text he uses the present tense which emphasizes an enduring or continuous action. This is difficult to translate into good, smooth English, but what the Apostle is saying, quite literally, is "you *be being kept filled*" with the Spirit, a continuous process which is repeated again and again in the experience of the child of God. This filling does not bring him into a new relationship to God, nor does it give him a new position before God. But it does relate to the believer's daily walk in relationship to the Spirit of God. When we say that this is experimental and is to be the continuous experience of all believers, we do not mean that this is a second work of grace, or some second added experience one is to seek for, or pray for, or meet certain conditions to obtain, as though God reserved it for a special few. Rather, it is the privilege of every child of God to be constantly filled with the Holy Spirit of God.

If you consider the teaching in the Book of Acts on the filling of the Spirit, you will notice that the same disciples were filled again and again. For instance, all those who were gathered together in the upper room on the day of Pentecost were "filled with the Holy Ghost . . ." (2:4). But Peter, who was one of those in the upper room on the day of Pentecost, was filled again (4:8). And the believers, who had previously been filled with the Spirit, were filled again as they heard of the report of Peter's conflict with the Sanhedrin (4:31). Stephen was chosen because he was a man full of the Holy Ghost (6:3), but just before he was martyred for his testimony for Jesus Christ, Scripture records he was filled again (7:55). Paul and Barnabas on a number of occasions were repeatedly filled with the Holy Spirit (9:17; 11:24; 13:9, 52).

A person was born into the family of God and that new birth by the Holy Spirit was never repeated. A person was sealed by the Holy Spirit once and for all and it was never repeated. A person was baptized into the body of Christ and it was never repeated. The Holy Spirit came to indwell the believer in the Lord Jesus Christ and it was never repeated. But this great work of the Spirit of God in filling the child of God might happen again and again and again. Every day that we live ought to bring us a new experience of this infilling of the Holy Spirit of God. Therefore we do not ever come to the place where we feel that we have arrived, that is, that we suddenly have become filled with the Spirit so that there is no need for added fillings of the Spirit. We never reach some elevated spiritual plain where God has nothing more to do for us, where we have come to the end of our experience with the Holy Spirit of God. "Be being continuously kept filled with the Holy Spirit" is God's command.

Paul brings up what seem to be two contradictory experi-

ences in order to teach us something about the unknown realm
from something we know. The Apostle emphasized the fact
that when one is drunk with wine, this drunkenness produces
a different kind of life and walk. That which wine produces,
in our King James version, is said to be "excess" (Ephesians
5:18). The word translated "excess" is the word for "riotous-
ness" or "rowdiness." One who is drunk with wine, or intoxicated with an alcoholic beverage, finds that alcohol has
so completely controlled and dominated him that it has produced an entirely different kind of a life. The man may be
meek and mild, a veritable Casper Milquetoast, but when he
is controlled by alcohol he wants to take on the world and
he is ready to fight anyone who comes along. You may never
get him to open his mouth in song when he is sober, but
under the influence of alcohol he wants to sing at the top of
his voice. He may seem to have no ability at all, but when
he is under the influence there is nothing that he won't try.
Do you get the point? Alcohol transforms the person. When
the apostle talks about being filled with the Spirit, he proceeds to show that one who is under the control of, or the
influence of, the Holy Spirit, will find that the controlling
Holy Spirit produces an entirely different kind of life. The
man is different, not because of what he is himself, but because of the power to which he has submitted himself and
the Person to whom he has yielded control.

What does the apostle have in mind when he says, "be
filled with the Spirit?" This word "filled" may be used in
two different senses. In the original text there are two different Greek words, both translated "filled." One seems to suggest a "filling up," as you might take a glass and a pitcher
of water and pour the water from the pitcher into the empty
glass so that water fills up the glass. That truth is related to

the indwelling ministry of the Holy Spirit. The disciples, on the day of Pentecost, were filled, that is, they were filled up with the Holy Spirit: the Spirit moved in, came in to dwell, and His presence was manifested in the believers. But the second word seems to have the added thought, not only of presence, but of power that manifests itself through the individual who is filled up. The word is used of sails that are filled with the wind. Now the result of filling sails with wind is that the boat moves. The sails are not truly filled with the wind when the wind simply billows them out, but they are, in the full sense, filled with the wind when the boat is moved, or carried along by the wind that is in the sail. In this Scriptural sense, when the Apostle Paul is talking about the filling of the Spirit, he is talking not only about the Spirit dwelling in a person, but about the added thought that the One who indwells *moves* the one who is filled into a new course of action, and produces a new kind of life.

This can be illustrated in the upper room discourse, when our Lord takes the disciples aside and emphasizes the truth that He is to be taken away from them, that He is going into death and that there will be a subsequent resurrection (John 16). But death and resurrection meant a separation from them. Our Lord says, ". . . because I have said these things unto you, sorrow hath filled your heart" (v. 6). What does it mean to have a heart filled with sorrow? When sorrow controls a person, it dominates him, and produces a new countenance, a new life, a new outlook. If we would understand what Paul is trying to teach us in Ephesians 5:18, in place of the word "filling," or "filled," use the word "controlled." We would not be amiss and it would make plain what Paul says: "Do not be drunk with wine, which produces riotous living, but be controlled with the Spirit which produces psalms, and hymns, and spiritual songs; it produces giving of thanks; it produces submission." So the Apostle brings this contrast to us to teach us that, as a man may yield himself to control by alcoholic beverage and find that it produces a new walk, a new talk, a new speech and a new manner of life, so the one who presents himself to control by the Holy Spirit of God finds that the Spirit produces a new walk, a new speech or talk, and a new manner of life.

There are certain prerequisites to this filling. A person who is grieving the Holy Spirit by any unconfessed sin, that is, a person who is out of fellowship with the Lord Jesus Christ because of that unconfessed sin, cannot expect to be controlled by the Holy Spirit of God. It is necessary for the Spirit to do a convicting work in the child of God who is living in unconfessed sin and the Spirit will not convict and fill, or control at the same time. The one makes the other impossible. In the strictest sense of the word, there is but one condition for the control by the Holy Spirit, or the filling by the Holy Spirit. Again we must refer to the illustration the Apostle uses. An individual may possess a bottle of a very intoxicating beverage. He may have purchased it and brought it into his home, but that possession will never bring him under the influence of alcohol. It is the act of submitting to the point of imbibing that alcohol which produces the control by the alcoholic beverage. In like manner, one who possesses the Holy Spirit will never be filled or controlled by the Spirit of God until that individual consciously submits to control by the Holy Spirit.

We belong to God by purchase. Because of the blood redemption, we are God's purchased possession. But God will not move into a man's life and force Himself upon him. Until an individual voluntarily submits to control by the

Spirit of God, he will not be filled and controlled by the
Spirit. This gives importance to such passages of Scripture
as, "I beseech you therefore, brethren, by the mercies of God,
that ye present your bodies a living sacrifice, holy, acceptable
unto God, which is your reasonable service" (Romans 12:1).
The words "that ye present" refer to the act by which the child
of God acknowledges God's right to do with him what He
wills. This is the act in which one disclaims ownership of
himself, discounts all rights to himself, and acknowledges
God's ownership and God's right to him as a person.

This same truth is presented when Paul says, ". . . yield
yourselves unto God . . ." (Romans 6:13). The word translated
"present" in Romans 12 is now translated "yield." I personally do not like the word "yield" because it suggests in-
voluntary submission to an overpowering force or influence.
I prefer the word "submit," or the word "present." So the
Apostle says, "Neither yield ye [or, present ye] your members
as instruments of unrighteousness unto sin . . ." (6:13). The
tense here is very interesting in the original text, for Paul is
literally saying, "Stop submitting or presenting your members as instruments of unrighteousness unto sin." He recognizes that that is exactly what people had been doing and he
calls upon them to stop. "Stop presenting, or submitting, your
members as instruments of unrighteousness but, once and for
all, present yourselves unto God." We sometimes refer to
this as consecration, sometimes as dedication, but it refers
to that moment of time when the blood-bought child of God
renounces his right to himself, his own way, his own desires,
his own strength, his own intellect and mind. He says "I am
no longer mine, but I am His." Paul was emphasizing this
truth when he said, "I am crucified with Christ: nevertheless
I live; yet not I, but Christ liveth in me . . ." (Galatians

2:20). Not *I,* but *Christ* liveth in me. When the individual says, "I accept God's will for my life, whatever it is, whenever it is revealed, wherever it takes me, once and for all," God's will becomes the determining principle in his life. That act is the presenting or yielding necessary for the filling of the Spirit. There are many of God's children who have never experienced the fullness of the Holy Spirit in their lives, day by day, because they never have come to the place where they are willing to surrender their own wills, their own way, their own wisdom, their own goals, ambitions and desires, to say, "Lord, I am stepping down off the throne of my life, and from this moment on I am acknowledging Your right to my life, to take it and use it as You see fit."

There is another part of this truth which is inseparably related to what has been said. Paul viewed the daily life of one who had presented himself to God, and he said, "Know ye not, that to whom ye yield yourselves servants to obey, his servants ye are to whom ye obey; whether of sin unto death, or of obedience unto righteousness?" (Romans 6:16). Paul recognizes that when the child of God makes this once-and-for-all decision to present himself as a living sacrifice, life then consists of a multitude of individual steps, to be taken one at a time, and God is the One who is guiding each individual step. It is the responsibility of the child of God to submit, not only once and for all, to the will of God, but to keep on submitting to daily manifestation of the will of God as they are made known. God has not seen fit to make His will known for every day of our lives at one time. He reveals His will day by day, moment by moment, step by step, and the individual child of God will never understand the daily steps of the will of God until, first of all, he has agreed to accept God's will, whatever it may be. Many of God's children are in constant turmoil because every time there is some new manifestation of the will of God they begin to debate, "Will I do it? Or won't I do it?" How easy it is, if a decision has previously been made to submit to God's will, to accept what God sends. And the life of rest, and the life of peace is the life that accepts God's will, whatever it may be, and waits for Him to reveal the individual steps along the way.

The opposite of submission is given to us in I Thessalonians 5:19: "Quench not the Spirit." We can not extinguish the Spirit, as though we could remove His indwelling presence from our lives. Quenching the Spirit means saying "No" to the manifestations and revelations of the will of God for each step along the way. Every child of God is living each moment submitting to control by the Spirit of God or rebelling against control. The individual who is in rebellion against the will of the Spirit of God is quenching the Spirit, and the individual who consciously submits to control by the Spirit is being kept filled with the Spirit. In many books on the ministries of the Spirit of God this matter of control by the Spirit, or the filling of the Spirit, is made such a complicated process that I don't see how anybody could ever know the joy of it. Yet God's truth concerning the filling by the Spirit is so simple.

Scripture reveals some of the consequences of a life that is lived under the control of the Holy Spirit of God. The Apostle tells us (Galatians 5:16) that if we walk by the Spirit we will not fulfill the lust of the flesh, and he speaks of the nine-fold fruit of the Spirit (v. 22). The result is a life of righteousness. We sometimes speak of this as progressive or experimental sanctification. Sanctification in the daily life is the product of the Holy Spirit living His life through the child of God. The Apostle also tells us (I Corinthians 2:9-10) that instruction is the result of being controlled by the Holy Spirit. God has a great body of truth to present to His children. It is referred to as "the deep things of God" (v. 10). That which men can't see, or hear, or reason in their hearts, the Spirit of God reveals.

Control by the Holy Spirit will produce guidance: "as many as are led by the Spirit of God, they are the sons of God" (Romans 8:14). Paul is relating the leading of the Holy Spirit to the filling of the child of God. Or, "The Spirit itself beareth witness with our spirit, that we are the children of God" (v. 16). The one who is filled with the Spirit has the assurance of his sonship with the Father. The Apostle shows us that all acceptable worship is the result of the filling by the Holy Spirit, for when the Spirit fills the individual, he will be speaking in psalms and hymns and spiritual songs, and making melody in his heart to the Lord (Ephesians 5:19). When God's people are controlled by the Spirit of God, they pour forth songs of rejoicing.

An acceptable prayer life is the result of control by the Holy Spirit, for "the Spirit also helpeth our infirmities: for we know not what we should pray for as we ought . . ." (Romans 8:26). God has promised to answer any prayer that is according to His will. How can we be assured that what we pray is according to His will? If it arises from our desires we have no assurance at all, but if we are praying under the control of the Holy Spirit we know He will not prompt us to pray for something contrary to God's will.

The Apostle shows us (I Corinthians 12:5) that God gives gifts to men so that the Spirit of God might energize the men to produce acceptable service. When we look at this great truth, we can see that the things that are most precious to us in our daily experience are directly related to control by the

Spirit: our daily walk in righteousness before the Lord; our understanding of the truths of the Word of God; our guidances in God's will for us in each step of the day; our assurance that we are in the place of blessing, that we are in the family of God; the worship that comes from our hearts to the Lord; the prayer that we are burdened to pray to move the hand of God; and the service that the Spirit prompts, day by day.

13

THE PERMANENT GIFTS
OF THE SPIRIT

THE APOSTLE PAUL, WRITING TO THE CORINTHIANS, FACED THE same problem that many in the church face today: the problem of ignorance concerning spiritual gifts. He said, "Now concerning spiritual gifts, brethren, I would not have you ignorant" (I Corinthians 12:1). He was dealing with a subject about which they *were* ignorant, and he wanted to dispel the existing ignorance. We could understand it this way: "Concerning spiritual things, brethren, I would not have you to continue in your present state of ignorance." A great deal of the confusion and disorder in the life of the assembly in Corinth arose because of their basic misunderstanding of the gifts of the Spirit. As we approach this subject which is of such vital importance in relation to the ministry of the Word of God and the part that each individual has in the ministry, we have divided it into two studies. We want to consider first the permanent gifts of the Spirit, and then consider the temporary gifts of the Spirit.

Scripture presents to us the fact that it is a ministry of the Spirit to dispense spiritual gifts. We recognize that there are men who are naturally gifted, or talented; who by birth have a higher intelligence quotient and abilities which put them head and shoulders above other men. But when we speak of the gifts of the Spirit, we are not speaking about the native talents with which certain individuals have been endowed by natural birth. We are speaking of a supernatural endowment.

There are two extremes which we face today as we come to the subject of spiritual gifts. On the one hand, we are faced with abuse. We find that the subject is suspect for many people because of the abuses and excesses arising from some teachings concerning spiritual gifts. Most of us could cite examples of fanaticism which have arisen around this doctrine. On the other hand, because the doctrine has suffered from abuse and excess, it has been neglected, and the average child of God does not know the teaching of the Word of God in the matter of spiritual gifts. Lest he be deemed a fanatic, or be thought to run to the same excesses to which many have gone in the quest for spiritual gifts, the average child of God shies away from the teaching of the Word of God. We want to steer a middle course between excess and neglect.

The Word of God recognized two kinds of gifts: permanent and temporary. Some gifts were designed to operate as long as the church has its existence upon the earth; other gifts were designed to be temporary in duration. If one puts emphasis upon that which was divinely designed to be temporary, and seeks to make those temporary gifts the norm for spirituality in a day when they do not operate, he will be led into disillusionment or to some fleshly excess which manifests a pseudo-spirituality.

There are two separate purposes which God had in view in giving gifts to the church. Some gifts were given for edification; that is, they were given that through their use the body of Christ might be built up. Paul says (Ephesians 4:11-12) God "gave some, apostles; and some, prophets; and some, evangelists; and some, pastors and teachers; For the perfecting of the saints, for [or, unto] the work of the ministry, for the edifying of the body of Christ." We see the same thing in verse 15: "speaking the truth in love, may grow up into him in all things. . . ." The Apostle emphasizes the fact that Christ is the head, and from the head the whole body has been fitly, or neatly, joined together, just as the finger fits to the hand, and the hand fits to the wrist, and the wrist fits to the arm, and the arm so neatly fits into the body. Your finger is held to your hand by tendons and muscles so that there is no division between the finger and the rest of the body. Paul is saying that the whole body of believers has been so intricately joined together, and compacted, or united, by that which every joint supplies, according to the effectual working in the measure of every part (every part contributes something to the total welfare and well-being of the body), and because this is true, the body increases into the building up of itself in love. The Apostle emphasizes that there are some gifts given for the building up of the body of Christ, so that there shall be no deformity, division or lack in that body.

There are some other gifts that are designed to be signs to substantiate and corroborate a message that has been given. Concerning the gift of tongues, (I Corinthians 14:22), the Apostle writes, "Wherefore tongues are for a sign, not to them that believe, but to them that believe not. . . ." The permanent gifts are for building up the body. They are primarily in relationship to believers, although not entirely so. On the other hand, the temporary gifts were essentially sign gifts that had a ministry to unbelievers rather than to believers.

All gifts that are given to the church, whether they are permanent or temporary, whether they are for edification or for signs, are based on the victory of the Lord Jesus Christ at the cross. Paul says, ". . . unto every one of us is given grace according to the measure of the gift of Christ" (Ephesians

4:7). Put the word "grace" and the word "gift" together and you will observe that the apostle is writing about certain grace gifts, gifts that were graciously bestowed by the Lord Jesus Christ.

Now, the question arises, On what basis did the Lord Jesus Christ have the right to give gifts to men or to the church? Paul says, "Wherefore he saith, when he ascended up on high, he led captivity captive, and gave gifts unto men" (v. 8). This expression "led captivity captive" has produced many different interpretations. There are those who believe that the phrase refers to Satan; that is, Christ, in His resurrection, led captive the one who held men captive—Satan. We recognize, on the authority of the Word of God, that Jesus Christ did enter into combat with Satan at the cross, and that a judgment was pronounced by God upon Satan. At the cross Jesus Christ was the victor over Satan. This however does not seem to be Paul's thought here; it is foreign to the context.

There are those who believe that the phrase should be understood in the sense that Jesus led captive those who were held captive; that is, Jesus Christ, at the time of His resurrection, led into freedom those who were in Sheol, or Paradise, awaiting an entrance into heaven. There is reason to believe that this is Scriptually possible.

There is still another interpretation that would be acceptable. The phrase could be a reference, not to a person, as the first two interpretations suggest, but rather to a principle, so that Jesus Christ triumphed over sin and death and that He leads into His glorious freedom those who before were in bondage to sin and death. I am not going to try to settle the problem as to which of these three interpretations is best, but rather I will point out the fact that before one can distribute any spoils from the battle, he has to be the victor in the battle. Whether the victory in this passage was over Satan; whether the victory had reference to Sheol, Hades or the grave; or whether the victory was over sin and death, we recognize that Jesus Christ did enter into conflict with all of these, and He was the victor over all. Because Jesus Christ is victor, He has the right to distribute the spoils that He has gained in His victory. The Apostle is not so much interested in defining the vict*im* as he is in pressing the fact that Jesus Christ is the vict*or*. What the Apostle is affirming is that Jesus Christ, at the cross, has triumphed over every enemy. He has been declared by the resurrection to be the victor. As the victor, from His throne, He may dispense gifts according to His good pleasure, and one of the first gifts He asked of God the Father to be given to men was the gift of the Holy Spirit.

A fact which must be emphasized is that all gifts are sovereignly bestowed by the Holy Spirit. Refer again to Paul who says, ". . . concerning spiritual gifts, brethren, I would not have you be ignorant" (I Corinthians 12:1). If you look at the text, you will observe that the word "gifts" is in italics, showing us that "gifts" is not in the original text. Correctly translated, it would read, "Concerning spiritual things," or, "concerning things related to the Spirit, brethren, I would not have you to be ignorant." The Apostle emphasizes the fact that there are diversities of gifts, but the same Spirit. Whether it be the gift of apostleship, or the gift of prophecy, or the gift of tongues, or the gift of healing, the same Holy Spirit is the One who has given these gifts to men: "But all these worketh that one and selfsame Spirit, dividing to every man severally [or individually] as he wills" (v. 11).

Spiritual gifts are not to be sought by men. A man does not receive a spiritual gift because he prayed for it, because he sought it, coveted it, trained for it. Spiritual gifts are a sovereign bestowal apart from the will or the inclination of the individual. The recognition of that fact immediately dispels a great deal of the excess and abuse attached to false teaching on spiritual gifts. There are many people who have tarried after meeting, and prayed and begged and shed tears to receive some spiritual gift—in all sincerity, but also in ignorance. You may object: The Apostle himself says, ". . . covet earnestly the best gifts . . ." (I Corinthians 12:31). Doesn't that negate what has been said? Not at all. The Apostle, in that passage, is speaking to the church and not to individuals. The assembly in Corinth were emphasizing the temporary "sign" gifts and neglecting the major "edifying" gifts. Paul is not writing to individuals to say, "You individuals covet a spiritual gift. He is writing to the whole assembly: "Put your emphasis on the edifying gifts, not the sign gifts."

Spiritual gifts are not an indication of the spirituality of the man who has been given the gift by the Holy Spirit. God does not give spiritual gifts to men in response to their spirituality. We need to emphasize that fact because we have fallen into the snare of feeling that if a man has been given a spiritual gift, it is because he is spiritually superior to other men. No spiritual gift may be properly exercised apart from a true relationship to the Holy Spirit of God, but spiritual gifts are not bestowed as rewards.

Spiritual gifts are the bestowal of the Spirit of God and sometimes the Spirit sovereignly picks out the most unlikely child of God and gives him a gift that, used by the Spirit of God, lifts him above all the natural abilities he ever had. That is the Spirit's way of working to make it known that what is produced is not from a man's natural ability.

Every child of God has *some* spiritual gift: "the manifestation of the Spirit is given to every man to profit withal" (I

Corinthians 12:7). The ladies need not be discouraged. Paul is using "man" here in the generic sense. Women are included, as well. "But all these worketh that one and the selfsame Spirit, dividing to every man severally [individually] . . ." (v. 11). Again, in Ephesians, the Apostle emphasizes the truth: "he . . . gave gifts unto men" (4:8). And to whom are these gifts given? "But unto *every* one of us is given grace according to the measure of the gift of Christ" (v. 7).

That fact immediately shows us that every individual who has been born into the family of God is essential to the body. In Ephesians, Paul was speaking about the welfare of the body as a unit, and we have all been made members in the body by the baptizing work of the Holy Spirit. God has given each one in the body a gift. While there may be different responsibilities in the discharge of the gift, each gift is essential to the total welfare of the whole body. Don't ever get the idea that you are unimportant. Joy in our Christian experience, and profit in our Christian ministry, depends on each individual recognizing his gift and using it. There may not be edification to the body if *you* try to exercise *my* gift; nor will there be edification to the body if *I* try to exercise *your* gift. But joy and blessing and success will depend on your knowing what your gift is and using that gift. If you discover that you have one spiritual gift, and wish that you had another one, and you neglect the gift that is in you, to do the work of another gifted person, that which you should be supplying to the body will be lacking, and there will never be edification. The Spirit of God must reveal to each one of us what our gift is. Then we must use that gift as the Spirit directs.

What are the permanent, or edifying, gifts? These are variously divided by different writers, but I suggest that there are eleven permanent, edifying gifts. The first (Ephesians 4:11)

is the gift of *apostle*. I must distinguish here between the
office and the gift. There were men who were appointed to
the office of apostle, and I do not believe that the office was
permanent. Only those could be apostles who had fellow-
shiped with Christ, who were witnesses of His earthly ministry
and His resurrection. The Apostle Paul was sovereignly appointed to the office of apostle, but the office was not a continuing or self-perpetuating office which could be transferred
by the laying on of hands. There is no such thing as apostolic succession. Apostle means *a sent one;* one who has been
sent out. It was the work of one who had the gift of apostle to
go into an area where Christ had not been named and to proclaim the truth of salvation through Christ, to bring a group
of believers together, to teach and train them, to establish
that nucleus of believers into an assembly or a church. It had
to do with salvation, and then edification, and then organiza-
tion. We find that the Apostle Paul gloried in his apostleship.
He recognized that he had the gift of an apostle and he would
go throughout the Roman world and preach Christ, gather
together believers, teach them, and then organize them into a
local assembly. I believe that this, in a sense, is a permanent
gift. When one goes into an area where Christ has never been
named and brings the message of the gospel so that a few of
those in darkness believe, and then teaches them, instructs
them, and organizes them into an indigenous assembly, that
man is doing the work of an apostle.

Along with the office of apostle was the gift of a *prophet*.
The prophet was one who spoke forth a message. The word
prophet means *to speak forth*. It also means *to foretell*. But
in the Word of God, the prophet was principally one who announced God's message. Remember that the prophets were
ministering when Scripture had not yet been completed. They

were men who received truth from God and could speak that truth for God to believers who had been established into churches by an apostle. They took the truth that had been revealed and brought it to people. Today, one who authoritatively proclaims God's Word is doing the work of a prophet. Of course, with the completion of Scripture, new truth is not revealed, but revealed truth may be proclaimed.

The third gift mentioned in Ephesians 4 is the gift of an *evangelist*. An evangelist had the particular gift of preaching the gospel to unsaved men so that they would hear and believe. This is a continuing gift to the present day. There are men who have an incisive knowledge of the Word of God, who stand up before an audience of the unsaved, and are doctrinally correct as they preach Christ, but they give the invitation and nothing happens. Is there something wrong with their doctrine? No. Another man preaches Christ and there is great response. What is the difference? One has the gift of evangelist and the other doesn't.

The fourth gift is the gift of a *pastor-teacher*. Commonly this is understood as two different gifts, but the words ought to be hyphenated. There is one gift: pastor-teacher. There will be two emphases in the ministry. As a pastor, he cares for the flock. He guides, guards, protects, and provides for those under his oversight. As a teacher, the emphasis is on the method by which the shepherd does his work. He guides, he guards, he protects by teaching. We teach the truths of the Word of God so our flock will not fall prey to error. In so doing we have discharged the gift of pastor-teacher.

In I Corinthians 12 Paul mentions the gift of *teaching*: "God hath set some in the church, first apostles, secondarily prophets, thirdly teachers . . ." (v. 28). The teacher of this verse is not identical with the pastor-teacher of Ephesians 4:11.

This is the gift of being able to take a newborn babe in Christ and teach that babe truths of the Word of God. This gift can be exercised in a Sunday school class or a home Bible class. When somebody comes to you and says, "I wish I knew something about the Word of God," and you take your Bible and turn to a passage and teach that hungry babe some truth from the Word of God, you are doing the work of a teacher. The pastor-teacher had a ministry to an assembly of saints, and this teacher may have a ministry to only one in the discharge of his gift.

Paul mentions also the gift of *helps* (v. 28). You might translate this as "the gift of ministry." The gift of helps is the gift of being able to assist. It includes the unseen ministries that contribute to the total welfare of the body.

Paul includes the gift of *administration* (I Corinthians 12: 28), or the gift of government, which concerns governmental oversight of the flock. The elder, to whom the spiritual oversight of the flock has been entrusted, has the gift of administration, or supervision. This includes not only instruction, but discipline as well.

In Romans 12:8, there is a reference to *exhortation*. The exhorter is one who has the ability to appeal to the will of the individual to get him to act. The teacher primarily presents truth, and the exhorter complements the work of the teacher and gets the one who has been taught to act on the truth. For instance, a teacher teaches from I John that we ought to love one another. The exhorter follows, saying, "Let us love one another" (I John 4:7). He is exercising the gift that supplements the gift of teacher.

Then there is the gift of *giving* in Romans 12:8: "he that giveth, let him do it with simplicity. . . ." Giving is a spiritual gift. Spiritual giving is not related to your bank account; it is related to the supervision of the Holy Spirit over you and your bank account. That is why it is called a spiritual gift.

Paul mentions, ". . . he that showeth mercy . . ." (Romans 12:8). This gift of *showing mercy* has reference to meeting the miseries of the poor, the sick, the afflicted; widows and orphans; those in physical or material need. It is the ability to sympathize with, or suffer along with another; the ability to put an arm around the shoulder and comfort and console. This is not human kindness, but a spiritual gift.

The last comes to us from I Corinthians 12:9: "To another faith by the same Spirit. . . ." Then Paul says, ". . . though I have the gift of prophecy, and understand all mysteries, and all knowledge; and though I have all faith . . ." (I Corinthians 13:2). He is referring to the gift of *faith,* which differs from the faith given to every child of God. The gift of faith is given to certain individuals, and with it they may lay hold of God in a special way. There are those to whom we would almost instinctively turn to have them pray for us when there is some great need pressing upon us. We recognize that they have the gift of faith, a laying hold of God in some special way which differs from the faith that every believer has.

No one man can or does possess all eleven gifts. No one man can or does possess enough gifts to discharge the work of building up the body of Christ all by himself. The Holy Spirit brings into the body of Christ, or into an assembly of believers, sufficient gifted ones so that through the operation of each gifted man the total work of the assembly might be carried on and the body edified. No church can succeed on a one-man ministry. The church can know the blessing of God and be edified in the things of God only as each gifted one in the assembly of believers contributes to the assembly what he has been gifted by God to do.

There is one question that remains unanswered. You want to know what your gift is! It is the ministry of the Spirit not only to give gifts, but to let us know what they are. Several suggestions will help us know our gift. The Spirit, first of all, gives us an inner inclination in the area of our gift. God would not give a man the pastor-teacher gift without creating a desire to manifest that gift. There are also many men who desire to be pastor-teachers but are not gifted. However, our gift will be recognized by the assembly of believers, perhaps before it is ever recognized by us. If you feel that you have a gift and you try to exercise it and nobody in the assembly indicates that you have that gift, then it is quite evident that that is not your gift. There should be the public recognition. I had been in my first pastorate just a matter of months when some people came to me and said, "You are a teacher. You ought to be in a theological seminary." I laughed, yet that is where I am today. Somehow, they seemed to recognize that I had a gift that I had no idea that I possessed, and it was the public recognition that authenticated the fact of the gift.

The blessing of God will be upon the ministry of your gift. When God gives us a desire, and there is a public recognition of that gift, and His blessing comes upon the administration of it, and we can then be certain that it is the gift God has given to us.

14

THE TEMPORARY GIFTS
OF THE SPIRIT

THE GREAT MAJORITY OF THE CHRISTIAN CHURCH IS EMBAR-
rassed by the phenomena practised by certain groups. Many
have come to feel that divine healing, speaking in tongues
and the like must be manifestations of a spirituality which we
do not possess. Because the teaching of Scripture concerning
these spiritual gifts is not known, these manifestations have
become tests of spirituality or proofs of control by the Spirit
of God.

There is a difference of opinion concerning some of the
gifts of the Spirit which we have chosen to include under the
heading permanent gifts. Particularly, I speak of the gift of
apostle and the gift of prophet. There are many students of
the Scriptures who feel that these are temporary gifts, and I
recognize that there is a sense in which both the gift of apostle
and the gift of prophet could be included in this study of the
temporary gifts of the Spirit. The gift of apostleship might be
considered both temporary and permanent, at the same time.
The gift of apostle was permanent when it related to the ministry of the church in propagating the gospel. When one was
sent by God to bring a knowledge of the gospel to those who
have never heard, as a missionary today brings the gospel to
those in heathen darkness, he is doing the work of an apostle.
We recognize, from the New Testament, that there was the

office of apostle, and this certainly was a temporary office. Only those could fill the office of apostle who had been in company with our Lord during the years of His earthly ministry, and who were personal witnesses of the resurrection and of the resurrected Christ. With the death of those who had been in company with Christ, it would be impossible for the apostolic office to continue. We thus could classify the gift of apostleship as it relates to the office of apostle as a temporary gift.

We could also call the prophet both a temporary and a permanent gift. By that we mean there were certain aspects of the prophet's work which were of temporary duration; while other aspects of the prophet's ministry would be needed and provided by the Spirit of God throughout the church age. The prophet was one who delivered a message from God to God's people. In the Old Testament, the prophet came with the message, "Thus saith the Lord." Prophets were needed in the New Testament era because of the transfer from Judaism to the truths of Christianity. There was a need that men should be sent by God to those who had been related to God by the old covenant so that they should be taught the truths of the new covenant and the new order. There was also a need for a prophet to deliver a message from God before Scripture was completed. With the completion of Scripture, which was God's revelation to men, there was no longer a need for that aspect of the prophetic ministry. There was no longer need for one man to be sent from God, empowered by the Spirit, to reveal the truth of God to men because the truth of God was revealed and recorded by inspiration in the Word of God. Prophets were needed in the early era of the church's history because, before Scripture was completed, the church needed some authority in both doctrine and practice. What were they to believe? How were they to live? We do not need the office of a prophet today because we have the Scriptures. In that sense, the need for the prophetic ministry ceased with the completion of the New Testament Scripture. We recognize that there are many today to whom the Word of God has not come. There are multitudes who do not have one word of Scripture in their own language. When God sends a man to those people, that man is doing the work of a prophet until such a time as the Word of God can be delivered into their tongue. The prophetic office in I Corinthians, chapter 14, refers, first, to believers in the Lord Jesus Christ. It is a ministry of edifying believers. Paul says, "he that prophesieth speaketh unto men to edification . . ." (v. 3), and "he that prophesieth edifieth the church" (v. 4). When a prophet ministered to believers, so that believers could be edified, he was ministering one of the permanent gifts of the Spirit. Today, when one brings the truths of God to babes in Christ so that they are built up in the Lord and in the faith, he is exercising the permanent gift of the Spirit. But according to I Corinthians 14:24 the prophet might have a ministry to the unsaved: "if all prophesy, and there come in one that believeth not, or one unlearned, he is convinced of all, he is judged of all." This refers to the ministry of a prophet to an *un*believer. This has to do, primarily, with the temporary gift of the Spirit. And so, we are suggesting in these two areas, the prophet and the apostle, that the ministry might be both permanent and temporary.

In I Corinthians 12:28 we have a partial list of some of the spiritual gifts: "God hath set some in the church, first apostles [the word "first" here is a reference, not to the first that is mentioned, or the first in this list, but rather the *first* in importance. God has set some in the church *first* in importance: apostles], secondarily prophets, thirdly teachers. . . ." The apostle is of primary importance because he is the initial one who brought the truth of God to men who were strangers to the grace of God. The prophet is of secondary importance because he delivered the message of God to those who had been brought to God through the work of the apostle. The teacher is mentioned third because he takes the Scriptures, or the truths, revealed by the prophet to those who have been brought to the Lord through the apostle and teaches and instructs them, so that they may grow in grace and in the knowledge of our Lord and Saviour. These three, we have suggested, are permanent gifts, but Paul says, "after that [that is, in a place of secondary importance] miracles, then gifts of healings, helps, governments, diversities of tongues" (v.28).

The gift of miracles is a general term that includes a number of other spiritual gifts. The gift of healing, the gift of tongues and the gift of interpretation were parts of the gift of miracles. When the Apostle referred to the gift of miracles, he was referring in a general way to a number of other gifts. In order to understand the ministry of God through miracles, we must observe different periods in recorded Scriptural history when the gift of miracles was emphasized. There were four great periods in which miracles happened with frequency. First of all, the period of Moses; second, the period of Elijah and Elisha; third, the period of Christ and the Apostles; and fourth, the period of the Apostles in the early church following Pentecost. A miracle is a sovereign work of God, a manifestation of divine power, given to substantiate and corroborate a message from God. Miracles were never performed to be spectacular; they were never performed to attract people to the miracle worker; they were performed to authenticate, to substantiate, to corroborate a message from God. The first great miracle worker recorded in Scripture is Moses. His miracles were performed in reference to the redemption of the children of Israel out of Egypt. When God would deliver the people of Israel from Egyptian bondage, Moses was given the power to work miracles for the benefit of Pharaoh. In Exodus 7:3 we find the statement of God: "I will harden Pharaoh's heart, and multiply my signs and my wonders in the land of Egypt." Notice that God says, "these are *My* signs and *My* wonders." It was not what Moses was doing, but what God was doing through Moses. "But Pharaoh shall not hearken unto you, that I might lay my hand upon Egypt, and bring forth mine armies, and my people the children of Israel, out of the land of Egypt by great judgments. And the Egyptians shall know that I am the Lord, when I stretch forth mine hand upon Egypt, and bring out the children of Israel from among them" (v. 4-5). How would Pharoah and the Egyptians know that God was working on behalf of the children of Israel? By the signs and the miracles that came through the hand of Moses who was given the power to work miracles not only for the benefit of Pharoah, but also for the benefit of the children of Israel. God has delivered the children of Israel unto the leadership of Moses, but how would the Israelites know that Moses was God's appointed ruler and leader? By the miraculous signs that came from the hand of Moses. In this first great period of miracles, the miracles substantiated Moses as God's appointed ruler for Israel and attested to Pharaoh the fact that God was moving on behalf of Israel.

In the second great period of the manifestation of miracles we come to the experience of Elijah in the contest between him and the prophets of Baal. There is a manifestation of miraculous power as the fire came from God out of heaven and consumed that water-soaked sacrifice which Elijah had offered (I Kings 18). We find the reason for this miracle: "it came to pass at the time of the offering of the evening sacrifice, that Elijah the prophet came near, and said, Lord God of Abraham, Isaac, and of Israel, let it be known this day that thou art God in Israel, and that I am thy servant, and that I have done all these things at thy word" (v. 36). The miracle was designed to have a two-fold lesson: it would substantiate the authority of God ("let it be known . . . that thou art God") and, it would authenticate Elijah as God's appointed representative. The miracles of Elijah and Elisha came in a day of Israel's apostasy to authenticate the message of judgment that came from their lips as being God's message. The prophets were sent to call a disobedient, rebellious people back to God. Both the messenger and the message were authenticated by the miracles.

The third great period of the manifestation of miracles is the period of Christ's ministry on the earth. In Luke 11:20 we have a statement about the significance of Christ's miracles. Christ had cast out a demon who had produced dumbness in the demon-possessed individual. Christ said, ". . . if I with the finger of God cast out devils, no doubt the kingdom of God is come upon you." Christ, in His earthly ministry, had presented Himself as Israel's king, and had offered to Israel the fulfillment of their kingdom promises. The miracles of Christ substantiated the Person of Christ, and authenticated the kingdom offer.

If you turn to Matthew, you find our Lord chose Twelve. He sent them out to minister. And "when he had called unto him his twelve disciples, he gave them power against unclean spirits, to cast them out, and to heal all manner of sickness and all manner of disease" (10:1). The power to work miracles was given to the disciples. Why? ". . . as ye go, preach, saying, The kingdom of heaven is at hand. Heal the sick, cleanse the lepers, raise the dead, cast out devils: freely ye have received, freely give" (v. 7). The miracles wrought by the disciples were to authenticate their message that Jesus was the Messiah, the Son of God, who had come to redeem Israel and to reign over that nation as David's son.

In each of these three cases the miracles were worked against a background of unbelief and they were designed to be a sign to unbelievers, whether it be the unbelieving Pharaoh, or the Egyptians, or the unbelievers in the nation Israel.

When we come to the fourth period of the manifestation of miracles, in the Book of Acts, we find that the miracles were wrought for exactly the same purpose. Anticipating the advent of the Holy Spirit and the ministry of believers to the world through the Spirit's power, our Lord said. ". . . these signs shall follow them that believe; In my name shall they cast out devils; they shall speak with new tongues; They shall take up serpents; and if they drink any deadly thing, it shall not hurt them; they shall lay hands on the sick, and they shall recover" (Mark 16:17). When the Apostle Paul came into Corinth, and his apostolic authority was questioned by enemies who followed him into that city, Paul proved, by the miracles he wrought, that he had come with divine authority. He said, "Truly the signs of an apostle were wrought among you in all patience, in signs, and wonders, and mighty deeds" (II Corinthians 12:12). The word translated "signs" is the word translated elsewhere as "miracles." In each instance of a multiplicity of miracles, the miracles were designed for unbelievers; they substantiated the messenger and the message as having divine authority and, therefore, being trustworthy.

The gift of miracles in any age seems to have been a temporary gift. With the completion of the New Testament Scriptures the authentication of any messenger ceased to be the miracles which he could work. The authentication became witness of the Holy Spirit to the truth the messenger taught. That is why the Apostle John, writing at the close of the Apostolic era, tells believers to "try the spirits . . ." (I John 4:1). Why? The test of any man's authority no longer was his ability to work miracles. His authority came from his adherence to the revealed truth of the Word of God. We do not originate a message, and by miracles authenticate a new revelation. We declare to you the message which has been completed. The Holy Spirit bears witness with our spirits that that which is preached is the truth of the Word of God. Thus miracles and signs no longer accompany the messenger.

Let it be very clear that God is still working miracles today, but there is a difference between working miracles and the gift of miracles. The one who had the gift of miracles, referred to in I Corinthians 12:28, could work a miracle at will. He could use that miraculous power whenever the need presented itself. But God is working miracles today in response to faith.

Let us consider several of the temporary gifts of the Spirit referred to in the New Testament. The first (I Corinthians 12:28) is the gift of healing. This gift has caused a good deal of consternation in many of God's children. We have certainly longed to see the gift of healing manifested when some friend or loved one has fallen sick. Much as we may desire the gift of healing at such a time, we are coveting a temporary gift.

There are certain fallacies in the divine healing movement. The first is the fallacy that physical healing has been provided by God in the atonement, or that healing is in the death of Christ. The favorite passage of Scripture used by the divine healers comes from Isaiah 53:5: "he was wounded for our transgressions, he was bruised for our iniquities: the chastisement of our peace was upon him; and with his stripes we are healed." The interpretation of all divine healers is that the word "healing" refers to physical or bodily healing. The fallacy of that will be evident to you immediately if you will read this passage in its context. Even in the verse in which that phrase occurs, you will find that the prophet is speaking, not about physical infirmity, but *spiritual infirmity:* infirmity of the soul. ". . . he was wounded for our transgressions; he was bruised for our iniquities. . . ." The chastisement that comes because of sin was upon Him. Isaiah was speaking about the infirmity of the soul which is healed by the death of the Substitute who died for us. If healing is in the atonement, we would like to ask the question, "Why does any child of God ever die?" Sickness ultimately culminates in death and death is the outgrowth of sickness. If healing is in the atonement, there could be no such thing as physical death. The fact that believers die negates this interpretation that Jesus Christ has died to remove all physical sickness.

A second fallacy commonly propagated by divine healers is that it is God's will for every man who is sick to be healed, or that it is not God's will that any of His children should ever be sick. Now this is contradicted by the Word of God, for the Word reveals to us that sickness and physical weakness is one of God's methods to get us to depend upon Him. The Apostle Paul prayed for deliverance from physical infirmity; he prayed again and again, and God said, "I won't remove it." Why? God wanted to teach Paul a lesson that he could learn in no other way. The lesson of conscious, moment-by-moment dependence upon God was learned by Paul through enduring physical sickness. The thorn in the flesh was something that taught him a truth. There is not one verse of Scripture that says that it is God's will that all should be healed; or that it is not God's will that any should ever be sick.

A third fallacy that has been very prevalent is that all physical sickness is the result of sin. God may use physical sickness to discipline us if we have sinned, or to bring us to a place of confession (I John 1:9). But that does not mean that all sickness is the result of sin. If it were, when the sin is confessed and dealt with we then could claim relief from the illness itself. It is on these basic fallacies that the divine healing movement is based.

Some of you will say, "But I know or have heard of people who profess to have been cured by divine healers, or have received some special physical blessing in a healing campaign." First, there are cures through some of these healing campaigns. Any doctor will tell us that sickness may be psychosomatic; that is, it may be produced by the mind of the individual. Any such psychosomatic illness may be removed by a suggestion from a divine healer. That is no miracle; that is the removal of the mental cause of the illness so that the illness itself can be taken away. Second, a great many so-called cures in a healing campaign are deliberate frauds to deceive the unwary who come in. Third, the supposed cures may be of satanic origin. Satan is the deceiver, and if he, by producing some physical cure, can bring men under his authority then he has gained a victory. The so-called cures may be attributed to one of these three causes: because the sickness was psychological; because the so-called cure was a fraud, or because it was a manifestation of satanic power.

According to Matthew, the power to work miracles was given to the disciples. They ministered that power. But I observe that this power was not a permanent gift to the disciples, for in Matthew 17:19, while Christ was on the mount of transfiguration, the disciples were confronted with a man in physical need, but they were not able to heal him. The power given to them in Matthew 10 was not a permanent gift. It was of temporary duration. When Christ would send out the seventy, at a later time, it was necessary for Him to give them the power to work miracles. And after the resurrection of Christ and the coming of the Holy Spirit, these disciples did not retain the power to heal which they had had previously. Some among them were given the power to heal, but the power was a temporary sign given to authenticate the messenger and the message. God, in response to believing prayer, does work miracles and we have seen many raised up as we asked God to heal, but it was not because we had the gift of healing, but because God is a God who can work miracles. If men have the gift of healing, there is only one place where it ought to be exercised: not in a tent, or auditorium to which the sick are invited to come, but in the hospital where the sick are. I've never known of a divine healer who came to a city to go up and down the corridors of the hospitals to dispense the gift he claims he has. It would be very hard to get a large offering there!

The next temporary gift is the gift of tongues, which was prophesied by Isaiah. It was to be a sign that God had sent a message that was to bring salvation to man. It is recorded (Acts 2:4, 8, 11) that on the day of Pentecost, the disciples spoke with tongues, that is, in other known languages so that men should hear the message that Christ had risen from the dead. The miracle of speaking with tongues takes place in the house of Cornelius (Acts 10:46) as, for the first time, the gospel goes outside of the bounds of Israel. And then (Acts 19:6) the gift of speaking in tongues is referred to again in an area where the gospel was preached outside of the land of Palestine and its environs. We would point out, as we did with the gift of miracles, that the gift of tongues was given to substantiate the messenger and authenticate the message. God did so by permitting men to speak, and by permitting other men to hear, in other known languages. This gift was a manifestation of supernatural and not natural power. It was produced by the Holy Spirit. It was not produced by psychological phenomena on the part of the speaker.

Where the Apostle speaks in detail concerning the gift of tongues (I Corinthians 14), we see no reason to distinguish his use of tongues from the use of tongues in the Book of Acts. These men were speaking, not in ecstatic utterance, but rather in languages that to them were unknown. There are a number of things that the Apostle has to say concerning the gift of tongues. We outline it briefly, and then commend this chapter to your extended study. First of all, we notice (I Corinthians 14:1-12) that the gift of tongues was an inferior spiritual gift. In fact, the Apostle seems to have put it at the bottom of the list of spiritual gifts. It was, in many ways, one of the most spectacular gifts, but in spite of that fact, it was classified by the Apostle as an inferior gift. Paul points out (v. 4) that the gift of tongues was not one that edified the saints; it was a gift that ministered to the speaker alone. It was, in essence, a selfish gift and because it was not one that edified, it was of secondary importance and value in the life of the assembly.

The second thing that Paul says about the gift of tongues (vv. 14-20) is that the gift should never be exercised unless there is an interpreter present. That is, there must be one who is able to interpret and explain the utterance, so that through the interpretation there shall be edification for the assembly. The temporary gifts are subordinate to the permanent gifts that would edify the body of Christ. In the next place, (vv. 21-22) Paul speaks of the intent of tongues. Why were they given? He says (v. 22) ". . . tongues are for a sign, not to them that believe, but to them that believe not. . . ." It was to convince unbelievers that divine authority was manifested in the assembly. And (vv. 23-40) Paul gives instructions concerning the use of tongues and he has six things to say. First of all (vv. 23-26), the gift of tongues is to be exercised decently, so that unbelievers may be convicted and believers edified. Second (vv. 27-28), you must have an interpreter. Third (vv. 29-30), you must restrict the number of people who speak in tongues at any one meeting. There would be confusion if they all spoke at the same time, or the meeting would be unduly lengthened. The fourth thing that the Apostle says (v. 31) is that they must prophesy in order, or speak in order, one by one. This prevents confusion. The fifth thing (v. 38) is that tongues must be controlled. Paul says here that the spirits of the prophets are subject to the prophets, and he means that if a man loses control over himself then there is a psychologically produced phenomenon and the manifestation is not produced by the Spirit of God. The spirit of the prophet must be controlled according to the will of the prophet so that all things shall be done in order. In the same way, Paul says, the women are to keep silence in the church. That has to do with the control in the use of tongues. If the women want to know something, let them ask their husbands at home. But the last thing that he says, (vv. 39-40) is that tongues are not to be prohibited in the assembly, even though they are of lesser order. Paul has had so much to say against tongues, and about the control of tongues, that he has to conclude by saying, "I don't mean that you never use tongues when it is a spirit produced gift."

Since the Apostle has so much to say about tongues, how can we say that the gift of tongues is a temporary gift? Paul tells us it is (I Corinthians 13). In the first eight verses the Apostle has been speaking on the gift of love, the manifesta-

tion of the love of Christ. He has described for us the out-
working of the love of Christ in the individual. He says (v.8),
"Charity [love] never faileth. . . . whether there be prophecies
[that has to do with the gift of prophecy in reference to un-
believers], they shall fail; whether there be tongues [that is,
the gift of tongues], they shall cease; whether there be knowledge, it shall vanish away." If these are temporary gifts, why
did God give them? Paul says (v. 9), "For we know in part,
and we prophesy in part." He says we are ignorant. Notice
that these gifts were associated with immaturity and ignorance: "But when that which is perfect is come [that is, full
maturity, full knowledge, full understanding of the revela-
tion], then that which is in part shall be done away. When
I was a child, I spake as a child, I understood as a child, I
thought as a child: but when I became a man, I put away
childish things" (vv. 10-11). And what Paul is saying is that
these gifts, and particularly the gift of tongues, were suited to
the infancy period of the church's history, but when the
church grew up out of its infancy, the members no longer
needed the substantiating and confirming sign of speaking in
tongues. If a church claims the need for the gift of tongues
today, it is confessing spiritual immaturity and ignorance of
the truth of the Word of God. The gift of tongues was suited
to the infancy period of church history before the Scriptures
were completed; before the Spirit had done His work of
teaching, instructing, revealing and illuminating the things
of the written Word. Tongues are not evidences of salvation;
they are not proofs of spirituality. Even in the era when
tongues were used in the church, they were gifts to the church,
and not all who were spiritual men had the gift. It was given
sovereignly to certain individuals. Like the gift of apostle,
the gift of prophet, the gift of pastor-teacher, it was a sovereign
bestowment apart from the spirituality of the individual.

The gift of tongues is not related to the baptism of the Holy Spirit. Here is the great fallacy of the Pentecostal movement that says the evidence of baptism by the Holy Spirit is that a man breaks forth into tongues. Every believer in the Lord Jesus Christ has been baptized by the Holy Spirit into the body of Christ and is a member of that body. Only a few individuals were gifted with the gift of speaking in tongues. All were baptized, but not all spoke. Thus, we would conclude that the gift of tongues was a temporary gift, designed to substantiate and corroborate. It had a ministry to unbelievers, but was not a gift which in itself would edify the church.

Parallel to the gift of tongues was the gift of interpretation of tongues (I Corinthians 12:10; 14:26-28). Paul says "If any man speak in an unknown tongue, let it be by two, or at the most by three, and that by course; and let one interpret" (14: 28). The word translated "interpret" here, is the ordinary word that is used for changing one spoken language into another spoken language so that the one can understand the thought of the other. The gift of interpretation of tongues is not the ability to take the ecstatic utterances that were vocalizations but not words, and to translate those vocalizations into some spiritual meaning. It was the translation of spoken words into another language. With the cessation of the gift of tongues, the gift of interpreting tongues likewise would cease.

The last of the temporary gifts is the discerning of spirits (I Corinthians 12:10). This may seem to contradict what John teaches (I John 4:1) when he tells us to "try the spirits," but there is a difference between "trying" the spirits and "discerning" the spirits. Believers today are instructed to try, or to test, the spirits. They test them by the written, revealed, inspired Word of God. But what were men to do before the Scripture was given by inspiration? God provided for the protection of the church by giving certain men the gift of discerning false teaching. They would listen to a man teach and know by the Spirit's gift that what was being taught was false teaching. With the completion of the Scriptures, we have the Scripture as the rule, the canon, the test of authority, and we need not the spiritual gift of discernment. But we need to discern.

With these spiritual gifts God made provision for the nurturing of the church in its infancy. Before the completion of Scripture, before the dissemination of the knowledge of the doctrines of Scripture, God gave men sign gifts. These gifts were exercised to the church but, more, they were exercised to those without the church, so that unbelievers might come to trust the man who came with a message from God. Today we do not look for these temporary gifts; we do not covet them as evidences of spirituality. We thank God that we no longer need the gift of healing, the gift of tongues, the gift of interpretation, the gift of discerning spirits. We have an authoritative Book which God has authenticated, and which we trust for teaching in doctrine and guidance in living.

The Apostle said to the Corinthians, ". . . covet earnestly the best gifts . . ." (I Corinthians 12:10). This was a word addressed to the whole assembly of believers. Paul did not say to individual believers that they should covet to be apostles, or prophets, or evangelists, or pastors or teachers. But he says to the assembly of believers as a whole, "You covet, in your midst, the ministry of these gifted men: apostles, prophets, evangelists, pastors and teachers; that through the exercise of all these gifts the whole assembly of believers shall be edified in the faith and shall be built up to the work of the ministry.

15

The Believer, the Spirit, and the Flesh

THE WORD OF GOD PLACES IMPOSSIBLY HIGH STANDARDS UPON the conduct of the child of God. We are commanded to walk as He walked, to live as He lived, to love as He loved. As we read through the Word of God and perceive the requirements which God lays upon those who have named the Name of Christ; we realize that we cannot, of ourselves, attain unto the standards which God has put before us. The recognition of this fact may lead one to despair. He may adopt the attitude that, since the standards for the Christian life are so high and so unattainable by human methods and human strength, it is pointless to try. There are others who, because of the standards of the Word of God, will be driven to the Spirit of God to cast their dependence upon the sustaining strength and grace of the Holy Spirit so that He may live His life through us.

We want to consider three areas in this general subject of walking by means of the Spirit of God: the believer, the Spirit and the flesh; the believer, the Spirit and the world; and the believer, the Spirit and the devil.

The Apostle Paul, writing to the Galatians, meets the problem of how a man can live a Christian life. Faced with the enemies of the world, the flesh and the devil, how can one measure up to that standard which God has set for His chil-

dren? There were those who had come into the assembly in
Galatia with the word that, while it was all right to accept
Jesus Christ as personal Saviour, if one were to attain to the
standards God lays down for His children, he needed something more than faith in Christ. They taught that it was necessary to add the works of the law to faith in Christ, and
affirmed that there would be no development in the Christian
life, there would be no progressive sanctification, there would
be no maturity apart from submission to and obedience of the
law of Moses. And it is this question to which the Apostle is
addressing himself. He reminded the Galatians that they were
redeemed by faith: "no man is justified by the law in the
sight of God, it is evident: for, The just shall live by faith"
(3:11). Quoting from the Old Testament a passage that was
written while the law itself was operative, Paul reminds us
that the Old Testament emphasized the fact that the just shall
live by faith: "And the law is not of faith: but, The man that
doeth them shall live in them. Christ hath redeemed us from
the curse of the law, being made a curse for us: for it is written, Cursed is every one that hangeth on a tree: That the
blessing of Abraham might come on the Gentiles through
Jesus Christ; that we might receive the promise of the Spirit
through faith" (3:12-14). In his first propostion Paul reminds
us that men were redeemed, not by the works of the law but by
faith, and that salvation is the gift of God to those who believe, to those who accept Him as a personal Saviour.

Paul states a second great principle; namely, that we became
the sons of God not by works, but by faith. He says, ". . . when
the fulness of the time was come, God sent forth his Son,
made of a woman, made under the law, To redeem them that
were under the law, that we might receive the adoption of
sons" (4:4-5). The word *adoption* has to do with placing one

in a position of privilege and responsibility. By special divine
appointment we, who were redeemed, were adopted or appointed to all the privileges and prerogatives that belong to
the sons of God. "And because ye are sons, God hath sent forth
the Spirit of his Son into your hearts, crying, Abba, Father.
Wherefore thou art no more a servant, but a son; and if a
son, then an heir of God through Christ" (vv. 6-7). Paul states
that we became sons of God, not by works of the law, but by
faith in the Lord Jesus Christ.

On the basis of that, Paul teaches his readers that there
were some, who had been redeemed by faith and made sons
of God, who were reverting to the law as a means of sanctification or as a means of progress and development in the Christian life. He says, "...after that ye have known God, or rather
are known of God, how turn ye again to the weak and beggarly elements, whereunto ye desire again to be in bondage?"
(v. 9). Paul is saying that those who have been redeemed and
made sons of God by faith, who have known God and are
known of God, have been enticed away from the faith principle and brought back under bondage to the law; not in
order that they might save themselves, for they have already
accepted Christ, but they, by submitting to it, sought to grow
in grace and in the knowledge of our Lord. They who seek
maturity by obeying the law, Paul says, are turning again to
the weak and beggarly elements. The very things from which
you were redeemed by grace, and grace alone, you desire to
be in bondage to once again.

The Apostle proceeds (Galatians 4:19-31) to draw a lesson
from the Old Testament to illustrate the danger of submitting
to the law. To Abraham were born two sons. One, Ishmael,
was born of the energy of the flesh; the other, Isaac, was born
by faith. And Paul refers to the Old Testament where it was

written in the Book of Genesis that God gave Abraham the commandment, "Cast out the bondwoman and her son: for the son of the bondwoman shall not be heir with the son of the freewoman" (v. 30). The principle that Paul draws from this analogy is that the works of the flesh did not bring Ishmael into blessing, nor did the energy of the flesh produce the fulfillment of the divine promise. The divine promise was fulfilled in Isaac, the one who was born of faith. Thus Paul illustrated the danger that confronts the Galatians, saved men who were reverting to the works of the law to bring themselves to maturity in Christ. The Old Testament showed that the child of faith received the promise, but the child of the flesh was rejected. Paul wanted them to see the principle that if they tried to reach maturity in Christ by the works of the flesh, they would miserably fail, and would have nothing of the maturity which they desired. But if they walked by faith, they would receive the promise, as Isaac received the promise.

Further, the apostle shows that maturity in Christ, or sanctification in our daily experience, is not to be attained by the energy of the flesh through keeping the law, or by doing good things. A man is not sanctified by his own power, nor by his own will, but by the faith principle. Paul develops his thought by telling us that those who seek to be justified by the law are fallen from grace (Galatians 5:4). The Apostle is not saying that those who seek to be justified in their daily life by the law have lost their salvation. Such would be contrary to the general teaching of the Word of God. But Paul says that if you were saved by grace, if you were redeemed by grace, if you became a child of God by grace, and yet you try to live the Christian life by your own strength, power and will, you have left the grace principle which redeemed you and made you a son of God. There are two principles by which a believer may live his life. He may live by the power of the flesh, or he may live by the power of God, through faith. The one who seeks to live his Christian life by the law lives by the power of the flesh, and is doomed to failure because his life can be no stronger than he is, and we, admittedly, are spiritual weaklings. But the Apostle says that if one lives the Christian life by the power of the Spirit of God, there will be victory and triumph, for he is living, not by the law, but by grace and by the power of the Holy Spirit. The Apostle emphasizes the necessity of the faith principle, for he says, "... in Jesus Christ neither circumcision availeth any thing, nor uncircumcision; but faith which worketh by love. Ye did run well [we could translate: You began to run well]; who did hinder you that ye should not obey the truth?" (v. 6-7). By going back under the law, in the belief that by the energy or will of the flesh they could live a life pleasing to God, they have denied the truth grace brings. Paul tells us, "... ye have been called unto liberty . . ." (v. 13); namely, liberty from the law. And he concludes his argument by saying, "This I say, then . . ." (v. 16). Those words give us the summary of all that Paul has been teaching since the third chapter. Through this extended section he has been building up to this one great principle or proposition. The conclusion of his teaching concerning the believer's relationship to the law for his experimental sanctification is: "Walk in the Spirit, and ye shall not fulfill the lust of the flesh" (v. 16). The world translated *walk* is a most interesting word because it suggests continuous and progressive action. Read it that way and you will get the full force of what Paul writes: "You be continually walking by means of the Spirit, and ye shall not fulfill the lust of the flesh."

The words "in the Spirit" may not bring the full meaning to our minds that Paul intended, for he is not saying, "you walk in the general sphere of the things of the Spirit, and ye will not fulfill the lusts of the flesh." That certainly would be true, but a far stronger teaching is: "You be walking by means of the Spirit." ". . . by means of the Spirit" points out the support or the strength by which a man walks. I don't believe I ever see a man who has a limb in a cast, or one who has to take each step with crutches, without this verse coming to mind very graphically, for the man who has suffered an injury to a limb, so that that limb cannot support him, must find some other means of support, lest he fall. The spiritual principle is identical. We have no power of ourselves. We must depend upon something, or upon someone for support, and if we take our steps in conscious dependence on the support given by the Holy Spirit, so that we are continually walking by means of the support of the Holy Spirit, we will not fall. We will be manifesting the fruits of the Spirit; we will be manifesting the life of Christ as it is reproduced in the believer by the power of the Spirit of God. But just as soon as we depend on our own strength or trust our own will, we will go down in ignominious defeat and disgrace. Paul's exhortation, then, is: "You be continually walking by means of the Spirit, and ye shall not then fulfill the lust of the flesh." On the authority of the Word of God we can say that the only antidote to the life of the flesh is the life lived by the power of the Spirit of God. There is no other alternative. It is either the life lived by the flesh, or the life lived by the power of the Spirit of God.

As Paul expands this truth, he proceeds to show us the necessity for walking by the Spirit: "the flesh lusteth against the Spirit, and the Spirit against the flesh . . ." (v. 17)—a warfare has been declared between the flesh and the Spirit. It is a mutual antagonism, a mutual warfare, not a one-sided battle, and Paul further affirms: "these [that is, the Spirit and the flesh] are contrary the one to the other: so that ye cannot [or, ye may not] do the things that ye would" (v. 17). The Apostle is presenting to us the same truth that is presented in the Epistle to the Romans: the believer is engaged in a constant warfare. When man was born into this world, he was born with a human nature. It was the quality, or capacity, of the human nature to sin. The human nature cannot do that which is pleasing to God. It manifests itself in the fruits of the sin nature. And whether the Word of God refers to the nature with which a man is born as the sin nature, or sin, or the flesh, or the old man, or the Adamic nature, it brings to our attention this same basic fact; namely, that the nature of man is corrupt and cannot do that which is pleasing to God. Now, when one is born into the family of God, as Peter testifies (II Peter 1:4), he is given a new and divine nature. An entirely new capacity is given to the child of God by that new birth. The new nature can only do that which is pleasing to God as it is energized by the power of the Holy Spirit. The new nature can reproduce the life of Christ as the Spirit works through that new nature. And between these two natures, or two capacities, there is a constant warfare. It is to be questioned whether the old nature and the new will ever agree on any course of action, or word, or thought in the believer's life. There is no word that you speak, no thought that goes through your mind, no action that you will, to which both natures will consent. That is why the Apostle says, ". . . that which I [the old] do I [the new] allow not; for what I [the new] would, that do I [the old] not; but what I [the new] hate, that do I [the old]. If then I [the old] do that which I [the new] would not, I consent unto the law that it is good. Now then it is no more I [the new nature] that do it, but sin [the sin nature] that dwelleth in me. For I know that in me (that is, in my flesh,) dwelleth no good thing: . . . the good that I [the new] would I do not: but the evil which I [the new] would not, that I [the old] do" (Romans 7:15-19). There the Apostle testifies of the warfare, unceasing and unremitting, that goes on within the breast of the child of God.

As the Apostle speaks concerning *the flesh*, he is bringing before us a very broad concept presented in the Word of God. The word *flesh* is used in a number of different ways. It is used in reference to the material body of man, and in that sense it has no ethical or theological implication at all. Our Lord referred to His body after the resurrection and said (Luke 24:39): "handle me, and see; for a spirit hath not flesh and bones, as ye see me have." Flesh referred to the material body of our Lord.

When *flesh* is used in an ethical and theological sense, it always refers to that part of the natural man which is evil in the sight of God. Look, for instance, in Romans 4:1, where we find that *flesh* is used of natural efforts on the part of man, independent of God: "What shall we say then that Abraham our father, as pertaining to the flesh, hath found?" That is, "What did Abraham get all by himself without God's help?" Why, he got nothing. There, *the flesh* speaks of the effort of Abraham apart from God. Again, in the Epistle to the Galatians, Paul says, "Are ye so foolish? having begun in the Spirit, are ye now made perfect by the flesh?" (3:3). *Flesh* refers again to the effort of man, apart from or independent of God. Again (Galatians 6:12), Paul says, "As many as desire to make a fair shew in the flesh, they constrain you to be circumcised. . . ." *The flesh* speaks of natural effort, independent of God. One more reference will suffice: "we are the circumcision, which worship God in the spirit, and rejoice in Christ Jesus, and have no confidence in the flesh" (Philippians 3:3). *The flesh* refers to what man is, or can do, apart from God. Man can do nothing. When that meaning is applied to Galatians 5, where Paul says, "Walk in the Spirit, and ye shall not fulfill the lust of the flesh," we find that he is emphasizing the fact that it is natural for man to declare himself independent of God; it is natural for man to repeat the first sin of Satan and refuse to walk in dependence on, and obedience to, the God who made him.

But the *flesh* is also used in Scripture to emphasize the weakness and the helplessness of natural man: "I speak after the manner of men because of the infirmity of your flesh . . ." (Romans 6:19). The natural man is characterized by infirmity or weakness in reference to the things of God. Again, Paul writes, "I know that in me (that is, in my flesh,) dwelleth *no* good thing . . ." (7:18). Thus the word *flesh* is used of that which is weak, infirm and helpless, wherein dwelleth no good thing.

Further, this word *flesh* is used of the state of natural men: "For when we were in the flesh, the motions of sins, which were by the law, did work in our members to bring forth fruit unto death" (Romans 7:5). When the Apostle says "we were in the flesh," he does not mean we were in a human body, but rather that we were in a state of sin, and being in the flesh is the same as being in the state of sin. All these concepts emphasize the inability of the flesh to keep the law or to please God.

All of these ideas have reference to unsaved men, for *the flesh,* in the ethical sense, generally means *the unsaved.* But when you turn to Romans 7:14, we find that *flesh* is used to refer to the saved man who still possesses a sin nature. Paul says, ". . . we know that the law is spiritual: but I am carnal [or, to translate it more accurately, I am fleshly], sold under sin." Paul did not mean that he was an unregenerate man.

Rather, he was affirming the truth that even though he had been given a new divine nature, the old sin nature—the Adamic nature, the lawless nature—was still in him and would operate whenever it had an opportunity. So Paul says he is carnal, that is, fleshly, because of these two warring natures. Then, he points out to us that the flesh is that through which sin manifests itself in our lives. There are some sins that may be sins of the mind and have no outward manifestation. But whenever sin has an outward manifestation, it must manifest itself through the flesh. And Paul says, ". . . put ye on the Lord Jesus Christ, and make not provision for the flesh, to fulfill the lusts thereof" (Romans 13:14).

As we try to summarize the Scriptural concept of the flesh, we see that it points out natural effort, independent of God's help and assistance; it emphasizes the weakness, helplessness, infirmity of the natural man; man in his unregenerate state. It also reminds us that the child of God, even though born into the family of God, still possesses a fleshly nature, and that whenever sin manifests itself, it does so as the fruit of that fleshly, or sin, nature. When Paul says, "Be constantly walking by means of the Spirit, and ye shall not fulfill the lust of the flesh," he is saying that the one who walks by the Spirit will not manifest the weakness, the helplessness, the infirmity of an unredeemed man who walks independently of God and thus manifests the sin nature through the flesh.

We are told that freedom from the flesh comes only through the power of the Holy Spirit: "if ye be led of the Spirit, ye are not under the law" (Galatians 5:18). A number of different interpretations have been given to this verse. There are those who understand Paul's teaching to mean: "If you walk by means of the Spirit, the Spirit Himself will produce a work of righteousness in you so that you will not go back and try

to keep the law in order to fulfill righteousness"—control by
the Spirit will deliver one from the law. There certainly is
truth in that interpretation. We suggest that perhaps the
Apostle is saying: "If ye, the children of God, are led (that is,
walking by means of the Spirit), you are not under the law of
the fleshly nature that is seeking to work through you, so that
deliverance from sin in the believer's life depends upon conscious dependence upon the Holy Spirit of God to reproduce
the righteousness of Christ in him." Freedom from the flesh
comes not by an act of the human being, not by resolution
and determination not to fall into that sin again. It comes
not by promising God we won't repeat what has brought
shame to His name. Deliverance from the power of the sin
nature does not come by praying; it does not come by reading
the Word of God, although they might contribute to victory.
Deliverance from the power of the sin nature comes from conscious dependence upon the Spirit of God, which permits
Him to live His life through us to the glory of God.

Paul proceeds to outline the manifestations of the flesh. In
these verses (19-21) we have a catalog of sin so heinous that,
after we read it, we feel so contaminated by the very recita-
tion of these sins that we want to go and take a bath. There
are sins that are sensual; sins that are perversions of religious
things; sins that are selfish; sins of intemperance. The flesh,
the Apostle says, may manifest itself in the moral realm, the
social realm, or the religious realm. It may manifest itself
against others, or against the man himself. These sins manifest what the flesh is, and they are never pleasing or acceptable to God, under any circumstances!

Paul concludes this section by giving us the manifestations
of the Holy Spirit: "the fruit of the Spirit is love, joy, peace,
longsuffering, gentleness, goodness, faith [or, faithfulness],

Meekness, temperance [or, self-control]: against such there is no law" (22-23). The fruit of the Spirit is love, and the love of Christ will be reproduced by the Spirit through the new capacity of the child of God. The joy of the Lord Jesus Christ, the joy of perfect obedience to the will of the Father, will be reproduced by the Spirit through the child of God. The peace of Christ, which came to Christ because of His conscious dependence upon and submission to the will of a sovereign God, will be reproduced in the child of God by the Holy Spirit. The long-suffering, or the gentle patience, of the Lord Jesus Christ that never retaliated against all the animosity shown Him, will be reproduced in the believer by the power of the Holy Spirit. The tenderness of the Lord toward those in need will be reproduced in the child of God by the Holy Spirit. The goodness (not goodnesses, but the essential goodness) that belonged to the Lord Jesus Christ will be reproduced in the child of God by the power of the Holy Spirit. The faithfulness of the Lord Jesus Christ, unswerving obedience to every revelation of God's will, will be reproduced in the child of God by the power of the Holy Spirit. The meekness, or submissiveness, of Jesus Christ to the will of God, will be reproduced in the believer by the power of the Spirit. The self-control, or the self-discipline, of Christ will be reproduced in the child of God by the power of the Holy Spirit. The Christian life is the life of Christ reproduced in the believer by the power of the Spirit of God.

The Holy Spirit will not reproduce the life of Christ in the child of God unless that child is walking in conscious dependence upon Him. A constant warfare is going on in the heart and mind and will of every child of God, every moment of every day; unrelenting, unceasing warfare. The flesh is seeking to manifest itself and its fruits through you, and unless you are consciously and positively controlled by the Holy Spirit, the flesh is manifesting itself. There is no such thing as a neutral act, or a neutral thought, or a neutral word in the life of the child of God. That which is not produced by the Holy Spirit, is produced by the flesh. Every step you take, every word you speak, every action of your life not consciously controlled by the Holy Spirit is being produced by the flesh.

I had a very good friend who, some years ago, was stricken by crippling polio. For five weeks the doctors had despaired for his life, and it seemed as though his days were numbered when uremic poisoning set in. In a most miraculous way God caused that paralysis to recede, and bodily functions were restored. The uremic poisoning was alleviated and my friend's life was spared, but he was left with legs which were unable to support him. As he recovered from the effects of disease, he was able to be fitted with steel braces and equipped with heavy crutches. He learned to walk again. He had no strength or power whatsoever in his legs; he could walk only by consciously depending on the braces and the crutches. On one occasion, the main steel brace on his right leg snapped at the knee and, deprived of the support of his brace and having no power in himself to walk, he went down in a heap on the floor. His leg was broken. He had to be fitted with heavier braces. He learned again the lesson that he must walk in dependence on a means of support other than himself, and to this day he must take every step in conscious dependence on that external means of support. We have no ability to walk so as to please God. The only way that the life of Christ can be manifested in us is by our walking continually in dependence upon the Holy Spirit.

16

THE BELIEVER, THE SPIRIT, AND THE WORLD

NO MILITARY GENERAL WAS EVER ABLE TO CONQUER HIS ENEMY until he had first analyzed and understood the enemy. No believer will ever be victorious in his Christian life until he has correctly analyzed and understood the enemy we face. There are some things that are enemies to an individual because of the very nature of the things themselves. Poisons are deadly because of their essential make-up, and consequently are enemies to mortal man. There are some things that are enemies to men because of their overwhelming power, or the force with which they may crush. There are some things that are enemies because of the enticements that they put before an individual. And if one were to try to conquer an enemy that manifests himself in overwhelming power by taking an antidote to poison, he certainly would be defeated, for all of the antidotes to poison could not stop the avalanche of power. And if one were to be on guard against a deadly poison, but were not aware that the enemy might use subtle enticements and not poison at all, he likewise would go down in defeat.

We meet enemies of our Christian life on three fronts. We fight against the *flesh,* which is an enemy because of its essential nature or character. We fight against the *devil,* who is an enemy because of his overwhelming force, or power. We fight against the *world,* which is an enemy because it can seduce and entice with craft and guile. In a previous study, we considered the walk by the Spirit in relation to the flesh. There we saw the Spirit was our only safeguard against the essential nature which we harbor within us. Born as Adam's sons, we harbor within us Adam's nature. By nature we manifest the deeds of the flesh, the works of the flesh, which are an abomination before God. Only as we are controlled by the Holy Spirit of God, and walk in conscious dependence upon Him, can we be victorious over the enemy which is a danger to us because of it's essential nature, or character. In the second of this trinity of studies we want to survey a very broad subject to give you something of the Scriptural teaching concerning the world as the enemy of the believer.

The believer is commanded, first of all, by the God of the Word to separate himself from the world: "Ye adulterers and adulteresses, know ye not that the friendship of the world is enmity with God? whosoever therefore will be a friend of the world is the enemy of God" (James 4:4). James is emphasizing the incompatibility, the irreconcilability, which exists between God and the world, and between the believer and the world. John again gives the command, "Love not the world, neither the things that are in the world" (I John 2:15). And then John gives three reasons for his command. The first is the impossibility of mixing affections. He says, "If any man love the world, the love of the Father is not in him" (v. 15). It is not the Father doing the loving when the child of God loves the world, and the love of God is incompatible with love for the world. The second reason is the content of the world system: "For all that is in the world, the lust of the flesh, and the lust of the eyes, and the pride of life, is not of the Father, but is of the world" (v. 16). And John there summarizes the enticements of the world system: the world appeals to the flesh, to the eye and to the pride of life, all of which are under the condemnation of a holy and righteous God. John gives a third reason for his commandment in the transitory character of the world system: ". . . the world passeth away, and the lust thereof: but he that doeth the will of God abideth for ever" (v. 17). James teaches that friendship with the world is enmity against God. And John gives us the commandment of our Lord: "Love not the world. . . ."

In the familiar verses found in Romans 12:1-2, the Apostle gives his exhortation: "I beseech you therefore, brethren, by the mercies of God, that ye present your bodies a living sacrifice, holy, acceptable unto God, which is your reasonable service." The command follows: ". . . be not conformed to this world. . . ." The word "conformed" literally means "run in the mold of," or "Do not bear the imprint, the stamp of the world, upon you." But rather, "Be ye transformed by the renewing of your mind that ye may prove what is that good, and acceptable, and perfect, will of God." We need not tarry on this portion of the Word for we are familiar with the commands of Scripture that the child of God is to be separated from the world as a system.

We come to consider the character of the world, in order that we might understand exactly why Scripture commands that we should not love the world, but should be separated from it. At least four different words are translated from the original text by our English word "world." The first word *ge,* translated "world" or "earth," refers to the earth as a geographical location. Scripture does not use *ge* in the command. The injunction is not "Do not love the earth"; God is not forbidding us to enjoy His handiwork. The second word *aion* is frequently translated "world," but it views the world under the aspects of time; all that is included within time, the sum total of the periods of time. It is said in Hebrews 1:2 that Jesus Christ formed the world; that is, the time periods. But the prohibitions on love do not include this word. The third word *oikoumene*, refers to the world as the inhabited earth, and emphasizes the world of people. We are not forbidden to love the people upon the earth. In fact, if there is no love for them, there will be no declaration of the gospel to them. The fourth word *kosmos* is used in several different senses. *Kosmos* literally means "an ordered arrangement"; that which has been systematized, ordered or arranged. When it is used in a non-ethical, or non-moral, or non-theological sense, it becomes almost the equivalent of *oikoumene*, or "the inhabited earth." *Kosmos* refers to the world of people, on occasion. For instance, in John 1:9-10, this word is used: "That was the true Light, which lighteth every man that cometh into the world. He was in the world, and the world was made by him, and the world knew him not." There *kosmos* is used of the world of men, or the universe created by God. It is also used in John 3:16: "For God so loved the world [the *kosmos*], that he gave his only begotten Son, that whosoever believeth in him should not perish, but have everlasting life." And it is not in this non-ethical sense that we are forbidden to love the world.

In the New Testament there are three different usages of *kosmos* in an ethical sense. An understanding of these will give us the import of the teaching that we are not to love the world. First of all, since the word *kosmos* refers to an ordered, or arranged, system, this word referred to the organized system that is under the authority of Satan. Satan is its god or its ruler. In John 12:31 you find our Lord's words: "Now is the judgment of this world: now shall the prince of this world [*kosmos*] be cast out." Or again, in John 16:11: "The prince of this world is judged." There Satan is referred to as a world ruler, the ruler of this *kosmos,* which is an ordered, arranged system under his control.

We find, secondly, that the *kosmos* is the manifestation of the basic philosophy or the goal of Satan. The Apostle Paul says (I Corinthian 2:12), "... we have received, not the spirit of the world, but the spirit which is of God; that we might know the things that are freely given to us of God." Now he contrasts the spirit of the world with the Spirit of God. When he speaks of the spirit of the world, he is speaking of the dominating, compelling, driving force which controls the world. But, he says, "... the Spirit searcheth all things, yea, the deep things of God" (v. 10). God has a purpose; God has a program; and that purpose or program is summarized by the phrase, "the deep things of God." John speaks of the deep things of Satan (Revelation 2:24), and by comparing the two verses we find that there are diametrically opposed goals, aims, ambitions, philosophies and systems of thought; the deep things of God and the deep things of Satan. The deep things of Satan manifest themselves in and through the *kosmos* world system of which Satan is the prince, or the ruler, or the god. We find, further, that the *kosmos* world system is the channel through which the satanic program is developed. Just as the demons could not operate apart from a body, whether that of a man or an animal, through which they could express themselves, so Satan cannot manifest or accomplish his goal, his philosophy, or his desire apart from some channel through which he operates. Through the *kosmos* world system Satan attempts to impede the purpose of God. In Revelation 11:15 reference is made to "The kingdoms of this world ..." or the kingdoms of this *kosmos.* The

kingdoms in this present world are the means by which Satan
is seeking to accomplish his purpose.

We find that the *kosmos* system, under the rulership of
Satan, the prince of the world, has its own standards, its own
conduct, its own aims, ambitions and goals. In Ephesians 2:2
the Apostle reminds the converted Gentiles that in times
past "ye walked according to the course of this world, according to the prince of the power of the air, the spirit that now
worketh in the children of disobedience." Notice that the
Apostle says you walked "according to this world. . . ." Then
in a parenthical explanation he says, ". . . according to the
prince of the power of the air. . . ." To walk according to the
world, then, was to walk according to the dictates of the
ruler of this world, Satan himself. We find, first of all, that
when the *kosmos* is used in this ethical sense, it is used of an
organized system under Satan as its ruler, which is the expression of satanic philosophy, the channel of satanic pro-
grams, and has its own standard of conduct diametrically
opposed to God.

The *kosmos* world, in a second ethical usage, refers to
humanity, to the ungodly multitude of men who are alienated
from God and are therefore enemies of God. When the word
"world" is used in reference to men, it refers to men in their
enmity against God. For instance, the Lord said, "The world
cannot hate you; but me it hateth, because I testify of it,
that the works thereof are evil" (John 7:7). A *system* cannot
hate, and when our Lord says "the world hates me," He has
a different meaning for the word "world" than an organized
system. Here He is using the word "world" in reference to
men, and He says that men in the world are characterized by
their hatred of God. Or again, the Lord said, "If the world
hate you, ye know it hated me before it hated you" (John

15:18). Paul writes, "For after that in the wisdom of God the world by wisdom knew not God, it pleased God by the foolishness of preaching to save them that believe" (I Corinthians 1:21). In the first references we cited, the world of men was characterized by their hatred of God. Here, in Corinthians, the world is characterized by ignorance of God—the world, by satanic philosophy, did not know or come to understand God. Again, Paul says, ". . . when we are judged, we are chastened of the Lord, that we should not be condemned with the world" (I Corinthians 11:32). And there, the Apostle is emphasizing the fact that the world of men, in their enmity and in their ignorance, are under divine judgment.

The Word of God gives us a number of characterizations of men in the world system. First of all, in I Corinthians 1:21, the worldling is marked by his ignorance of God. That does not mean that the worldlings are without their gods. Many gods they have, but they are ignorant of the true God. Peter writes (II Peter 2:20) that the world is characterized by defilement: "if after they have escaped the pollutions of the world through the knowledge of the Lord and Saviour Jesus Christ, they are again entangled therein, and overcome, the latter end is worse with them than the beginning." I emphasize the phrase, "the pollutions of the world. . . ." From the divine viewpoint the world is polluted, or defiled. In II Peter 1:4, the Apostle states that there are "given unto us exceeding great and precious promises: that by these ye might be partakers of the divine nature, having escaped the corruption that is in the world. . . ." The world is not only polluted, but corrupt. There is a difference between an inactive poison and a virulent poison. The world is not only polluted in the sight of God, but there is an activity in the pollution that spreads the corruption. It is not dormant, but actively contagious, and that is the emphasis that Peter makes when he says we have "escaped the corruption that is in the world. . . ." Further, we find that the world is under judgment, and the worldling is under judgment along with the prince of this world. We referred earlier to John 12:31: "now shall the prince of this world be cast out." And when, at the cross, judgment was meted out upon the prince of this world, that judgment came upon all who are in the *kosmos* system. The Apostle John tells us that the world is under satanic control (I John 5:19): "we know that we are of God, and the whole world lieth in wickedness," or, as it might be literally translated, "the whole world is cradled, as a mother cradles her babe, in the lap of the wicked one." The world is under satanic control. Thus the world is marked by its ignorance of God; by it's defilement; by it's corruption; by the judgment under which it rests.

In the third place, *kosmos* refers to worldly affairs or worldly things. Joseph H. Thayer, one of our Greek lexicographers, defines this usage as "the aggregate of things earthly; the whole circle of earthly goods, endowments, riches, advantages, pleasures, etc., which, although hollow and frail and fleeting, stir desires, seduce from God, and are obstacles to the cause of Christ." The first use of the word "world" was in reference to a system. The second use was in reference to people in that system. Now the word "world" refers to the instruments used within that system by men. We would refer to them as worldly things. It was this to which the Apostle had reference when he said (Galatians 6:14), "God forbid that I should glory, save in the cross of our Lord Jesus Christ, by whom the world is crucified unto me, and I unto the world." What the Apostle said was that the worldly things that formerly enticed him, and which would normally entice a man, had no longer any appeal to him because he has died to worldly things. Again (I John 2:15-16), an Apostle says, "Love not the world, neither the things that are in the world," and he uses the "things of the world" to refer to the enticements that may come to the worldlings who are in the world system. Paul (Ephesians 2:2) reminds us that as we walk according to the course of this world, our life, day by day, is bent upon the things the world has to offer. When you consider this word "world" in it's ethical usage in the New Testament, it refers first to a system that is under the control of Satan and is the expression of the philosophy of Satan; when you see, in the second place, that it refers to men who are within the system of Satan; and when you see that it refers, in the third place, to the things that emanate from the god of that system, to keep men within the framework of that system, you can understand why the command of Scripture is given to us: "Love not the world."

Consider the relationship of the believer to the world. First of all, the believer has been taken out of the *kosmos*. Remember that he was born into the *kosmos;* he was a part of the kingdom of Satan; he was a worldling by birth. But the believer has been taken out of the world by a new birth. Listen to our Lord's words as, praying to the Father, He speaks of the disciples: "They are not of the world, even as I am not of the world" (John 17:16). Just as Christ belonged to heaven, even though He walked upon earth, so the believer has been translated out of this *kosmos* and he is no more a citizen of it than Jesus Christ was, even though He walked in the midst of it. Our Lord said, "If ye were of the world, the world would love his own: but because ye are not of the world, but I have chosen you out of the world, therefore the world hateth you" (John 15:19), emphasizing the great transition that has taken place. By natural birth they were in the world, but by a new birth they have been taken out of the world.

Not only has the believer been taken out of the world, but the believer, judicially, has been separated from the world. That is what the Apostle had in mind when he said he had been crucified unto the world and the world unto him (Galatians 6:14). The world may spread its baubles before a man and he may find them very enticing, but when death overtakes him the world may dangle its choicest baubles before him but they have no appeal whatsoever. He no longer has eyes to see; he no longer has ears to hear; he no longer has hands to reach out and to grasp and to hold to his bosom the things the world presents. And the Apostle was saying, "I died with Christ, and when I died with Christ, I, as one dead to the world, could no longer be enticed by the world." The believer has been judicially separated from the world and that was why the Apostle could write (Philippians 3:20), "our conversation [or our citizenship] is in heaven; from whence also we look for the Saviour, the Lord Jesus Christ." A transformation has taken place: we were born as citizens of this world, and we now have been made citizens of glory by the new birth.

We find in the next place that the believer has been sent by our Lord into the world, from which he has been taken out and judicially separated. In our Lord's prayer (John 17:11) He says, ". . . now I am no more in the world, but these are in the world, and I come to thee. Holy Father, keep through thine own name those whom thou hast given me, that they may be one, as we are." And (v. 18), "As thou hast sent me into the world, even so have I also sent them into the world." The Lord Jesus Christ never surrendered His rights to a place at the right hand of the Father when He was born into the world, when He became the incarnate Son of God. He said that as He belonged to heaven even though He was in the world, so the disciples no longer belonged to the world. Jesus sent them into the world that they might be as lights shining in the darkness.

Even though he is sent into the world, the believer is to keep himself from the world. In the first chapter of James, the Apostle says, "Pure religion and undefiled before God and the Father is this, To visit the fatherless and widows in their affliction, and to keep himself unspotted from the world" (v. 27). John again adds his testimony (I John 2:15): "Love not the world. . . ." The believer has been separated from the world by his death in Christ. He has been sent into the world to be a witness to the world, but he is to keep himself from the world. In a previous study we defined fleshliness or carnality as any manifestation of the fleshly nature of the individual. In like manner, worldliness is any conformity to the *kosmos* system of Satan. The difference between fleshliness and carnality is not so much what a person does, as the motivation for his actions. If an act originates from the desire of the flesh, it would be called fleshliness or carnality. If it is in response to the enticement from the world, it would be termed worldliness. It is not so much what a man does, as it is the origin of the enticement to the man, that gives us the distinction between worldliness and carnality.

How are we, as believers, to live in the midst of the world and keep ourselves unspotted from the world? In a very practical way, the Apostle writes: ". . . this I say, brethren, the time is short: it remaineth, that both they that have wives be as though they had none; And they that weep, as though they wept not; and they that rejoice, as though they rejoiced not;

and they that buy, as though they possessed not; And they that use this world [kosmos] as not abusing it: for the fashion of this world passeth away" (I Corinthians 7:29). There is found one of the first principles, laid down in Scripture, to govern the believer's life in relationship to the world. He is to use the world, but not abuse it. We would have to recognize that there is much in this world that is good, usable and useful. The believer is not asked to separate himself from that which might rightly be used, but rather to use it without abusing it. For instance, an automobile, or a radio may be used for a good purpose, or it may be put to a wrong purpose. It is the use to which the thing is put, not the thing itself, that is worldly. The problem in the believer's life, then, is to use, but not abuse, that which is in the *kosmos*. The believer must constantly sit in judgment upon all his thoughts, upon his desires and ambitions, and must bring every thought into conformity to the Lord Jesus Christ.

This brings us to the relationship of the Holy Spirit to the problem of the world in the life of the believer. Worldliness is essentially the problem of motives and affections. In back of this problem of affections is the problem of selfishness, or self-ness. We desire to cater to ourselves, and when we manifest our own nature with its desires, its goals, its aims and ambitions, we will readily fall prey to the enticements Satan will put before us, through the world, to wean our love away from the Lord Jesus Christ. The Spirit, then, must sit as the Governor and the Lord of our affections. That is why John writes, in reference to love, that the child of God must love not the world. The danger is that the Spirit of God will be deprived of His rightful control in the believer's life and the believer will prostitute the God-given capacity to love upon those things which God hates. That is why the Apostle

James says, "Ye adulterers and adulteresses, know ye not that the friendship of the world is enmity against God?" (4:4). An adulterer is one who is unfaithful to one to whom he has been joined in love. And the spiritual adulterer is the child of God who allows his love to be prostituted upon those things God hates. To give way to the enticements and blandishments that come to us from a system that is under satanic control, so as to be brought into conformity to the prince of this world instead of being conformed to the Lord Jesus Christ, is worldliness. And it is only as one's motives, goals, desires, pleasures and habits are brought under the control of the Holy Spirit that one can be delivered from this enemy who approaches us by enticements from without.

Paul gave us the secret as to how we could refrain from being conformed to this world. In Romans 12:2 he gives the command: "be not conformed to this world. . . ." Now what is the antidote to world conformity? It is found in the next phrase: "but be ye transformed by the renewing of your mind. . . ." The renewing of your mind is the operation of the Holy Spirit upon your thought process, your emotions, your will, so that the one who by nature would fall before the enticements of Satan through the world system is guarded by the Spirit and conformed to Christ. The Spirit causes us to repudiate those enticements and to be conformed to Jesus Christ instead of being conformed to the world.

"This I say then, Walk in the Spirit, and ye shall not fulfill the lust of the flesh" (Galatians 5:16). The secret of deliverance from the lust of the flesh is by means of a walk by the Spirit, or a walk in conscious dependence upon the Spirit. The only deliverance that the child of God has, the only safeguard against the enticements of the world, is found in conscious dependence upon the Holy Spirit of God. It is this thought that the Apostle James has in mind when he refers to our threefold enemy: he speaks of our old fleshly nature: "your lusts that war in your members" (4:1); he speaks of the world as an enemy of God (v. 4), and he speaks of the enemy, the devil (v. 7). And the antidote to this threefold enemy is: "Draw nigh to God, and he will draw nigh to you" (v. 8). Conscious, intimate relationship, continuous dependence upon the power of the Spirit of God, can blind us to the enticements of the world and bring us into conformity to the Lord Jesus Christ. Only as we understand our enemy, his methods, his goals; and only as we walk in conscious dependence upon the Spirit of God by the renewing of our minds, can we be conformed to Christ and separated from the world.

17

THE BELIEVER, THE SPIRIT, AND SATAN

IF WORD SHOULD BE RECEIVED THAT NEW YORK CITY WAS about to undergo an invasion by a foreign power we would expect the supreme command of the army, the navy and the air force to take every means available to protect that key city. Because the navy gave protection from invasion from the water, the army and the air force would not be warranted to withdraw protection against invasion by the land or the air. Should an attack come by water, that would be no reason to conclude that another attack could not come either by air or by land. There would be a need to defend the city from every source of attack.

We are fighting a threefold enemy: the world, the flesh and the devil. Because attacks are made against believers in the Lord Jesus Christ from one front, we have no right to assume that the enemy will always attack from that same front, and that we need not be on guard against the other avenues of invasion. The only defense against the enemy within, the flesh, is conscious dependence upon the Holy Spirit of God. The only defense against the enticements of the world is conscious dependence upon the Spirit of God. We come now to the third of the believer's great enemies, Satan. Let us consider the enemy, himself; then consider the exhortations to believers by which they may be protected from the enemy.

In Isaiah 14 and Ezekiel 28 it is recorded that Lucifer, the Son of the Morning, was the wisest and most beautiful of all created beings. He was given a position of authority over all the angelic creation. Yet, this one refused to remain in the position in which he had been placed by creation, coveted for himself the authority that belongs to God, and led a rebellion against God Himself. This one was transformed from Lucifer, the Son of the Morning, into Satan, or the devil, the infamous slanderer, the adversary, the lawless one. When Satan led the rebellion in which a multitude of angels followed, he became the prince of the power of the air. Paul says, "Wherein in time past ye walked according to the course of this world, according to the prince of the power of the air . . ." (Ephesians 2:2). The prince of the power of the air is Satan, or the devil. He is called the *prince* because he rules in a sphere, the *air*. He is the head of a host of angels who are his minions, who do his will in the execution of his lawlessness and rebellion against God. Our adversary, then, is no underling, but a prince who has assumed regal authority in his own realm.

Further, we find (II Corinthians 4:4) that Satan is referred to as "the god of this world," or of this age: "In whom the god of this world hath blinded the minds of them which believe not, lest the light of the glorious gospel of Christ, who is the image of God, should shine unto them." He has elevated himself to a position of prominence, not only in governmental spheres, but in religious spheres as well. He claims the worship that belongs to Almighty God, and causes men, through delusion in false religious systems, to worship him. It is significant that those who follow Satan do not necessarily become irreligious; nor do they become enemies of religion. They may become devotees of a religious system, but it is never a religious system that centers in the Lord Jesus Christ, nor one that recognizes the sovereign authority of Almighty God. It is a religious system that centers in Satan's counterfeit so that Satan may truly be called "the god of this world."

Satan always operates by deception. The Lord said that Satan is a liar and the father of lies (John 8:44). As such he will never operate according to truth. Remember that the Lord Jesus Christ is "the way the truth, and the life" (John 14:6). Truth centers in a person. Truth emanates from God. Truth is revealed from God to men through the Lord Jesus Christ, who is Truth. Satan operates in a sphere that is totally different from the sphere of God. Since God always operates in the truth, Satan operates in the opposite of truth, in the sphere of a lie or deception. Paul says that Satan operates by blinding the minds of men (II Corinthians 4:4). The mind is the faculty which receives truth, perceives it and as-similates it. If Satan would perpetrate a lie, he must first of all darken the perceptive powers of men so that they do not recognize his deception. In II Corinthians 11:14 Satan is transforming himself into an angel of light to deceive men into believing that he presents the truth when he is present-ing a lie. This is borne out in a passage such as Revelation 20:2-3, where an angel "laid hold on the dragon, that old serpent, which is the Devil, and Satan, and bound him a thousand years, And cast him into the bottomless pit, and shut him up, and set a seal upon him, that he should deceive the nations no more. . . ." The thing that characterized the work of Satan in this world was that he had deceived the nations. The nations had gone after "the god of this world," had fol-lowed "the prince of the power of the air," had become en-slaved in his iniquitous system, so that his deception has become their philosophy.

Our enemy never practices truth, nor is he ever forthright in the operation and the execution of his plans. Rather, he uses wiles to deceive, if possible, the very elect. In Ephesians 6:11, the Apostle is referring to this fact when he points out that we are to put on the "whole armour of God, that ye may be able to stand against the wiles of the devil." We do not expect that Satan will burst upon us with a frontal attack, for error seldom masses a frontal attack. Error insinuates itself into the mind by stealth, craft and subtlety. Therefore, our enemy is not one whose movements we can predict, nor can we know exactly what he will do because he appears to conform to truth. He is an enemy who moves by deceptions, deceits and wiles.

We find another interesting fact about our adversary from what is inferred in the Epistle of Jude: "Michael the archangel, when contending with the devil he disputed about the body of Moses, durst not bring against him [that is, against the devil] a railing accusation, but said, The Lord rebuke thee" (v. 9). This verse infers something of the power that belongs to Satan. Michael the archangel did not have sufficient power of himself to argue with Satan, but he had to call upon the power of God to defeat Satan in his desire to claim the body of Moses. If the archangel did not have power to stand against Satan, how can we expect to stand against him? Satan possesses a supernatural power, a power above that which is possessed by men.

Satan is an unseen adversary. He does not appear against us in flesh and blood. The Apostle says, "...we wrestle not against flesh and blood ..." (Ephesians 6:12). If we were wrestling against another man, we would know the vulnerable points in our adversary. But we are wrestling against principalities, against powers, against the ruler of the darkness of this world, against spiritual wickedness in high places. Paul teaches that Satan has an organized system of which he is the god and the head, and under him are organized lesser ranks of angelic beings, his demons. When we wrestle against him, we are wrestling against these unnumbered, organized hosts of powers which have their headquarters in high places, that is, in the heavenlies and not in this sphere in which we live. We are fighting enemies from outer space, if you please.

Our adversary is always bent on destruction. Peter writes, "Be sober, be vigilant, because your adversary the devil, as a roaring lion, walketh about, seeking whom he may devour" (I Peter 5:8). Because we were once within his kingdom, under his dominion, conforming to his standards and practices, and because we have been translated out of the kingdom of darkness into the Kingdom of God's Son, and have been born into a new family and have received a new standard of life and a new empowerment in that life, the one who formerly was our god and our ruler is now our adversary, bent on destroying those who have defected from his kingdom. You and I, as God's children, are viewed as guilty of treason by Satan. We have rebelled against his authority, we have come out from behind his "iron curtain." Consequently we are the special object of satanic attack. This is the kind of enemy we have to fight. As though it were not bad enough to have to fight against the enemy within, the flesh, and the enemy around us, the world, we have to add the enemy that is prince over all in this world system.

In view of the character of the enemy, we find some rather startling exhortations in the Word of God. We might have expected the Apostle to tell us to flee. When he wrote to Timothy, he said there are some temptations which the child of God has no right to try to withstand, or to fight against, and that the only thing he can do is to run when they put in their appearance. But Paul has told us to stand up against him and fight. The reason is that Satan is a coward. That is also inferred in I Peter 5:8: "your adversary the devil, as a roaring lion, walketh about, seeking whom he may devour." You probably thought when Peter made reference to a roaring lion he spoke of a power and fierceness that produced dread. But a lion is not most dangerous when he is roaring, for you know he is there. The lion is more dangerous when he is silently stalking his prey. The lion roars only after he has slain and is trying to impress all with his regal authority. The roar is essentially an act of cowardice.

Viewed from Scripture, Satan is a coward. He can be put to flight when one is willing to stand against him in the power of the Lord and make use of the provisions God has made. Notice what Peter told believers to do. He has warned them to be on guard concerning Satan's activities, to be sober [that is, serious-minded, considering the nature of the enemy, so as never to underestimate him], be vigilant [that is, be watchful, and don't ever feel that he is going to let you alone]. Then he says, "Whom resist stedfast in the faith . . ." (v. 9). The word "resist" was a military word that formed a command. As a military commander marched toward the enemy, he would command his troops, "take your stand!" Peter said that believers must take their stand against the adversary in the same way a soldier in the army would plant his feet, or take his stand, before the enemy.

In James 4:7 the same command is given: "Submit yourselves therefore to God. Resist the devil, and he will flee from you." There is no thought of turning and running, no thought of camouflage, of veiling your presence from the enemy by some deception. The only way to meet him is to meet him head-on; to take your stand; to plant your feet; to resist the devil so that he will flee from you.

If the child of God were given exhortations to meet this kind of enemy in his own strength or his own power, he certainly would go down to defeat. It would be pointless to tell a mortal being, in a body of flesh and blood, to try to do battle against a supernatural enemy who has such a bag of tricks at his disposal. But in Ephesians, Paul has described the equipment given to the child of God so that he might be able to stand: "Wherefore take unto you the whole armour of God, that ye may be able to withstand in the evil day . . ." (6:13). Now "the evil day" is any day in which you are attacked by the adversary. That would be every day, wouldn't it? Paul says, ". . . take . . . the whole armour of God that ye may be able to withstand. . . ." The word "withstand" is the same Greek word that is translated "resist" in James 4:7 and I Peter 5:9-10. So if we translate it the same way in each case, we find that Paul is saying, ". . . take . . . the whole armour of God, that ye may be able to *resist* in the evil day." We are able to resist this enemy only by putting on the equipment that has been given to us. No Roman soldier was responsible to provide his own equipment, it was provided for him. And any commanding officer would see to it that his soldiers were properly outfitted to meet the enemy in battle. When the Apostle speaks of "the whole armour," he is referring to the complete armor that would be given by a commanding officer to his soldiers. The inference is that God, our new Commanding Officer, has provided us with every piece of equipment, which it is necessary for us to have to go into the battle and come out unscathed. God is not primarily interested in winning a battle; God is interested in preserving the soldiers who belong to Him. Although the believers go into battle, God has made provision so that no believer need be lost in the battle. The panoply of God, the full armament of God, has been provided in Jesus Christ.

Let us look at the armament God has provided. Paul tells us to "Stand therefore, having your loins girt about with truth. . . ." (Ephesians 6:14). When any Roman soldier was going into battle, he would roll his long robe, which he customarily wore, waist-high, and bind it with a sash or girdle. This freed him for rapid movement. If he had worn the long, enveloping robe, he would have been hindered in his operations. First the soldier of Jesus Christ must remove that which would encumber. The writer to the Hebrews says (12:1), ". . . let us lay aside every weight, and the sin which doth so easily beset us, and let us run with patience the race that is set before us." While he uses the figure of the race track instead of the warrior, the thought is the same. The contestant must remove the encumbrance. The Apostle says that when one puts on the whole armor of God, he will begin by having his loins girt about with truth. The sword would be suspended from the girdle, so that this girdle would not only remove the encumbrances but would provide that from which the weapons were carried. The Lord Jesus Christ is Truth (John 14:6). The Apostle is not instructing believers to have their loins girded with that which is true, but rather, to have their loins girded with *Him who is truth.* The Lord Jesus Christ is the One who unites in Himself; the One who removes encumbrance; the One through whom and by whom weapons will be provided that may be used to withstand Satan in the evil day.

In the second place, the Apostle says, ". . . having on the breastplate of righteousness" (Ephesians 6:14). The breastplate, for the Roman soldier, was very much like a vest which covered the chest and abdomen. It might have been made of chain mail, or of overlapping pieces of metal, or of thick leather covered over with bone or horn. It was devised to protect the soldier from sword thrust by the enemy. The breastplate of righteousness frequently is interpreted as the righteousness of Christ. We certainly are covered over with His righteousness, and this is the basis of our victory over Satan. But the Apostle is dealing with the experimental side of truth, not the positional side. The breastplate of righteousness refers to the righteousnesses of the child of God. There is nothing that brings defeat so much as a guilty conscience. There is nothing that makes us want to turn tail and run so much as the conviction that there is unrighteousness within us. A conscience that is bearing the guilt of some unconfessed sin will turn the child of God into a coward who cannot withstand or resist the devil. There are many who go down to defeat daily before the onslaught of the enemy because they have not kept short accounts with God, and have not used I John 1:9 to "confess our sins . . ." so that He might be "faithful and just to forgive us our sins, and to cleanse us from all unrighteousness." We cannot go into the battle against the enemy, who is the accuser of the brethren, with some basis for his accusation, and come out as victors. We must have on the breastplate of righteousness.

The Apostle tells the believer to have "your feet shod with the preparation of the gospel of peace" (Ephesians 6:15). The Roman soldier went into battle wearing hobnailed boots instead of the light sandals which he ordinarily wore. They gave him a sure footing when he met the enemy in hand-to-hand combat. Unless his feet were secure when he made a sword thrust, he would surely go down and his adversary could make speedy work of him. The preparation of the

gospel of peace is not the peace with God that we have because we have accepted Christ; rather it is the peace that
is our daily portion, the settled assurance that we are in the
hand of God, and the knowledge that we can stand against the
adversary because He has given us the victory. When the
Apostle said, ". . . thanks be unto God, which always causeth us
to triumph . . ." (II Corinthians 2:14), he had his feet planted
solidly on a truth from which he could not be shaken. And
the child of God who has appropriated the promises of God,
and who has saturated his soul with the knowledge of the
Word of God, so that he knows he can stand against the
enemy, has his feet planted securely and he cannot be thrown
off balance. Before you can have your feet firmly planted
upon the promises of God, you must know the promises and
appropriate them. When you are in the thick of the battle,
it is too late to go thumbing through your Bible to find a
verse to stand on. You need to arm yourself with the truth
of the Word of God before you come into conflict.

The fourth piece of armor is the "shield of faith . . ."
(Ephesians 6:16). The words "above all" may mean "most
important of all," but the words are better understood as
meaning "over all," or "covering all." The soldier has put
on the girdle, the breastplate and the boots, but in front of
those he places the shield of faith. The shield was used not so
much to protect the person as to protect the armor that protected the person. It was double security, if you please. Before
the enemy's sword or fiery dart could pierce the breastplate,
it had to pierce the shield. And so, there was not only equipment and protection for the person, but there was protection
for the protection. Paul is saying, "Over all, taking the shield
of faith, wherewith ye shall be able to quench all the fiery
darts of the wicked." Many times the Roman army fought

against an enemy who would dip arrows into burning pitch, and from a relatively safe distance shoot them toward the adversary. The Roman soldiers were equipped with swords, but with swords it was rather difficult to meet the enemy who was shooting fiery darts from a distance. But the Apostle says that the shield of faith protects you from the enemy who is at a distance. This is not faith in the sense of faith in the Lord Jesus Christ as a personal Saviour, but rather it is this quiet confidence in God and God's sustaining grace, the faith that God is Victor and assures us of victory.

Paul refers to the next piece of armor as "the helmet of salvation . . ." (v. 17). The helmet covers the head, and the believer's knowledge that he is a child of God will be the protection for his mind. In writing to the Philippians, Paul says, ". . . whatsoever things are true . . . , honest . . . , just . . . , of good report; . . . think on these things" (4:8). The soldier who knows that he will go through that battle unscathed is going to be an entirely different kind of soldier from the one who momentarily expects to be killed. It is the knowledge that Christ will preserve us that guards our thinking, and this assurance comes to us from the fact that we have salvation.

Finally, Paul refers to the only offensive weapon, the sword of the Spirit, which is the Word of God. The Roman soldiers used two different kinds of swords. There were those who were trained to use a short sword, very much like a dagger, which could be used to pierce through the armor of the enemy. There were others who were trained to use a broad sword, a very long and heavy weapon which was grasped by two hands, raised over the head, and brought down upon the head of the adversary with a splitting blow. What the Apostle is emphasizing is the same truth presented in Hebrews 4:12: "For the word of God is quick, and powerful, and sharper than any two edged sword, piercing even to the dividing asunder of soul and spirit, and of the joints and marrow, and is a discerner of the thoughts and intents of the heart." The Word of God is incisive, cutting, penetrating, and it can defeat the adversary.

In Ephesians 6:18 the Apostle mentions the manner in which the weapons are to be used. Frequently this verse is listed as one more weapon. Rather, the Apostle is telling how all these weapons are to be used: the girdle of truth, the breastplate of righteousness, the shoes of the gospel of peace, the shield of faith, the helmet of salvation, the sword of the spirit. All are to be used "Praying always with all prayer and supplication in the Spirit. . . ." And that last phrase, "in the Spirit," gives us the power by which the weapons can be effective. Look at verse 10: "Finally, my brethren, be strong in the Lord, and in the *power* of His might"—and the Holy Spirit is the power of His might. Because our enemy has been described as a supernatural enemy who works by deception and guile and craft; because our enemy is an unseen enemy, so that we know not from which direction he is coming, nor how he is going to attack; and because we are exhorted to resist the devil, we need some supernatural power to be able to meet him. How can we meet an unseen enemy? How can we be wise to his subleties, crafts and deceits? How can we overthrow one who controls principalities, powers and rulers of the darkness of this world? We cannot, by ourselves. It is only as we walk in conscious dependence upon the Holy Spirit of God that there can be any victory over the devil. God has not given us the victory—He has given us the Victor. And we can have victory over our adversary only because we possess the Victor Himself.

The equipment is all that the child of God needs, but the child of God does not have the wisdom, or the power, or the strength to use the equipment himself. But there is One who dwells within the child of God who can use all the equipment by the power of His might. As we must walk by the Spirit to have victory over the flesh, and to have victory over the world, so must we walk by the power of the Spirit to have victory over our enemy, Satan.

18

IS THERE A SECOND WORK OF GRACE?

THE SPIRITUAL BLESSINGS THAT ARE OURS IN CHRIST JESUS are very much like the material wealth possessed by Solomon: "The half has not been told." Because of our limited ability to receive and understand the things of God, no matter how far we have gone into the depths of the truths of the Word, there are always unexplored depths. We understand the word of the Apostle Paul as he writes (I Corinthians 13:12): "... now we see through a glass, darkly. . . ." We are like the disciples of old whom our Lord had been teaching for the three and more years of His ministry. He concluded His teaching ministry saying (John 16:12), "I have yet many things to say unto you, but ye cannot bear them now." We are trying to encompass an infinite God with our finite minds, and we have to confess our inability to fathom the depths of the Person of God, the truths of the Word of God and the work of the Lord Jesus Christ on our behalf. We realize, as the children of Israel realized when they stood on the borders of the promised land, that there is very much land yet to be possessed.

We are always cognizant that there may be those who have entered into truths of the Word of God which we ourselves have never appropriated, and we have accustomed our ears to listen for spiritual truths and we have opened up our minds to receive that which God has revealed to His children out of the Word. And if someone comes to us and says that what we received in our salvation is only a part of the blessing that God has and that there is much more for a child of God beyond the salvation experience, we instinctively begin to wonder if there are things that we have missed, and if there are new experiences into which we may enter.

As we consider this question, "Is there a second work of grace?", we are face to face with one of the most prevalent, popular and fastest growing teachings in Christendom today. This teaching says that God parcels out His blessings, measure by measure, part by part; that one who has accepted Christ as Saviour may receive a second blessing from God, an experience that is akin to the first blessing of receiving salvation. This second blessing is to be the gift of the Holy Spirit. Those who would promulgate this teaching are motivated, without doubt, by a deep and sincere desire to go deeper into the truths of the Word of God, and to enter experimentally into the power that God has provided for His children. There is a heart hunger that motivates these seekers to desire the work of the Holy Spirit in their own lives, and they would tell us that when one comes to a certain state of maturity, or when one reaches a certain level of spiritual development, or when one is sanctified in his daily life, or when one enters into a deeper knowledge of the Word of God; that in response to his plea he may receive the second work of grace, the gift of the Holy Spirit. If there is such a thing as a second work of grace, if there is more than we have already experienced and possess, we certainly want to know it.

Without doubt the problems that arise around this teaching come from an interpretation of the Book of Acts where, when the Holy Spirit came to indwell believers, we have the signs associated with the coming of the Spirit, and we find the laying on of hands associated with the manifestation of the Spirit's presence in the life of the believer. So we shall examine some passages in the Book of Acts to see whether we are to seek the gift of the Holy Spirit as a second work of grace. Do we ask for the sign gifts to prove to us that we have the Spirit? Is this gift associated with the laying on of hands? If so, who can impose hands so that the Holy Spirit will come to take up residence in a believer's life?

We would remind you that the Book of Acts is the point of transition between the Old Testament and the New Testament. While, in our Bibles, the four Gospels are included with what we call the New Testament, everything before the Book of Acts is essentially the Old Testament. Christ had not yet offered Himself as the sacrifice for the sins of the world; Christ had not been buried and Christ had not been resurrected; the veil of the temple had not yet been rent in twain; God was dealing exclusively with the children of Israel as His chosen people. It is not until we come to the Book of Acts that we step from the old order, or economy, into the new economy after the death and resurrection and ascension of Christ; after the descent of the Holy Spirit, as it is recorded in Acts 2; after God had set aside a program that was restricted to the nation Israel and gave a message that was to go to the ends of the earth, to all men, irrespective of their race. In Acts we have the transition from Judaism to Christianity, from Jew to Gentile, from law to grace, from Palestine to all the world.

It is in the second chapter of the Book of Acts that we have the first reference to the coming of the Holy Spirit: "they were all filled with the Holy Ghost, and began to speak with other tongues, as the Spirit gave them utterance" (2:4). On the day of Pentecost the Spirit came to indwell God's new temple and a new era, a new economy, a new dispensation began, when the Holy Spirit baptized believers into the body of Christ to join them to that body with Jesus Christ as the head. In Acts 4:31 we find a reference to a ministry of the Spirit: "when they [the disciples] had prayed, the place was shaken where they were assembled together; and they were all filled with the Holy Ghost, and they spake the word of God with boldness." Those who were filled with the Holy Ghost in Acts 4:31 were essentially the ones who had received the Holy Spirit in Acts 2:4. The disciples were gathered together, privately, and they were again *filled* with the Holy Spirit, but this was not a second work of grace. They did not receive something that they had not received previously. The filling of the Holy Spirit in this second instance was a repetition of the Spirit's empowerment; the Spirit controlled them to enable them to preach and to proclaim the truth that they had been publicly announcing throughout Jerusalem. This is not a second work, but is a continuation of the work that had been begun in Acts 2. And those who were empowered to preach with boldness on the day of Pentecost, were again empowered to preach the Word with boldness. I call to your attention that in both instances the ministry was to the nation Israel. The proclamation of the gospel was made to sons of Abraham, the Jews, who were there in Jerusalem. The Lord, before His ascension, had told the disciples of the steps that would be followed in the proclamation of the gospel: "ye shall be witnesses unto me both in Jerusalem, and in all Judæa, and in Samaria, and unto the uttermost part of the earth" (Acts 1:8). There would be a ministry in and around Jerusalem: it would be the first step in the proclamation of the truth that Christ had died and had been raised again. Second, the Word would be proclaimed in Samaria: it was to go beyond those who were sons of Abraham to those who were of mixed heritage. And third, the gospel was to go unto the uttermost parts of the earth: beyond those who were Jews, beyond those of mixed heritage, to those who were Gentiles by race. In Acts 2:4 the Spirit empowered the disciples in the proclamation of the gospel in the first step of spreading the good news that Christ died for the sins of the world. The Holy Spirit filled or controlled them, and used them as His instruments to proclaim the truth of the Word of God.

Then the Word of God began to go outside the bounds of Jerusalem and Judea, beyond those who were Jews by birth to the Samaritan people who were a race of mixed lineage: "when the apostles which were at Jerusalem heard that Samaria had received the word of God, they sent unto them Peter and John" (Acts 8:14). Philip had been given the gift of an evangelist, and he had gone outside Jerusalem and Judea to exercise the gift to those who were of mixed heritage. According to Acts 8:12: "they believed Philip preaching the things concerning the kingdom of God, and the name of Jesus Christ, and they were baptized, both men and women." They had placed their faith in the Lord Jesus Christ and publicly announced their faith by being baptized. We have to realize that salvation, according to the Word of God, is of the Jews, and salvation to the Jews first was the principle upon which God had been operating. Now the church at Jerusalem heard the report of this work of God in Samaria, and the disciples wanted to know whether it was a genuine work of God among non-Jews, or whether it was some false teaching, a work of Satan rather than the work of God. So a delegation was sent from the believers in Jerusalem. Peter and John were sent to determine whether God was stepping outside the bounds of the nation Israel to bring salvation to other people.

When Peter and John arrived in Samaria, they "prayed for them, that they might receive the Holy Ghost: (For as yet he was fallen upon none of them: only they were baptized in the name of the Lord Jesus.) Then laid they their hands on them, and they received the Holy Ghost" (v. 15-16). That event appears to have been a second work of grace, for the Samaritans believed and it was not until some time later that they received the Holy Ghost. It may have been several days, perhaps a week, or even longer, before Peter and John came from Jerusalem to Samaria to investigate. When they got there they found that the Word of God had been preached in truth, for Philip was a Spirit-controlled evangelist, and would not, by the Spirit's control, preach falsehood. The people had genuinely accepted Christ; had attested their faith in Christ by public baptism. But they had no knowledge and no experience of the ministry of the Holy Spirit, for God had not yet done outside of Israel what He had done on the day of Pentecost. It was in connection with the ministry of the Apostles, through the laying on of hands, in response to their prayer, that there was a repetition of what took place in Acts 2 for the Samaritans. The Holy Spirit came to indwell non-Jews, and to join those outside of Israel into the body of Jesus Christ.

We may ask the question, "Why the laying on of hands in reference to the receiving of the Holy Spirit?" Let it be pointed out that this work was a work only for believers. Peter and John could have laid their hands on the head of all the unbelievers in Samaria but nothing would have happened. The Apostles, because they were given the office of apostle and the gift of apostleship, were given special authority by God. They were the instruments through which God worked in the transition out of the old order into the new. In the Old

Testament, when one laid hands upon the head of another, he was identifying himself with the one on whom the hands were laid. It was an act of identification. The priest identified the sinful people with the sin-bearing sacrifice by laying his hand on the head of the animal. When the Apostles placed hands on the heads of believers, they identified themselves with the believers, and those believers were identified with the Apostles' doctrine, with the Apostles' gospel, and with the Apostles' authority. These Apostles became the channel through which the Samaritans received the Holy Ghost. The Samaritans had not previously had any knowledge of the Holy Spirit or of the Holy Spirit's ministry; nor had the Holy Spirit historically put them into the body of Jesus Christ until this point of time. This, then, was a transitional experience, not a second work of grace. It was not something that was given to them because of their spiritual maturity—they were only a few hours old in Christ. It did not come to them because of their knowledge of the truths of the Word, or because of their experimental sanctification. God sovereignly used the Apostles as the instruments through whom the Holy Spirit came on the believers in Samaria.

In Acts 10 we find the record of the invitation given by Cornelius to Peter to come and declare the truths of God to him and his house. Cornelius was a Gentile. And now we observe a significant fact. In Acts 2 the Holy Spirit came on the Jews. In Acts 8 the Holy Spirit came on those who, by heritage, were non-Jews, or a mixed race. Now, in Acts 10, we have a ministry of God to those who were Gentiles according to the flesh. Peter proclaimed the truth of the Word of God to Cornelius' house: "While Peter yet spake these words, the Holy Ghost fell on all them which heard the word" (v. 44). Here the Spirit of God was repeating, for the third time, what

had happened on the day of Pentecost. This time it was not
to Jews, nor to those who might indirectly claim some blessing
because they were of part Jewish blood, but it was to those
who had no claim upon God through the Old Testament
covenant. They were Gentiles. Yet, as Peter was speaking,
because of their acceptance of the message the Holy Spirit
fell on all those who heard the Word. "And they of the
circumcision [that is, the Jews], which believed were astonished, as many as came with Peter, because that on the Gentiles also was poured out the gift of the Holy Ghost" (v. 45).
The Jews were amazed that God would save Gentiles and
would give them equal privileges and identical blessings. In
the Old Testament God had built a hedge around Israel. God
had said that the nation Israel was His people, His chosen
race. "Salvation is of the Jews" meant salvation is *for* the
Jews, as far as the Jews were concerned. The Gentiles were
called dogs. Dogs were unclean animals; they were scavengers
who lived outside the camp and consumed the refuse that was
put there. And now, God, in His infinite grace, was saving
Gentiles and, moreover, God was bringing them into the
same body as part of the same temple into which both those
in Judea and Jerusalem and those in Samaria had been
brought. The gift of the Holy Ghost was given to them. This
is so extraordinary that when Peter returned to Jerusalem he
felt compelled to make a report to the saints. He must defend
his action. Concerning his ministry in Cornelius' house. Peter
reports, ". . . as I began to speak, the Holy Ghost fell on them,
as on us at the beginning. Then remembered I the word of
the Lord, how that he said, John indeed baptized with water;
but ye shall be baptized with the Holy Ghost. Forasmuch
then as God gave them the like gift as he did unto us, who
believed on the Lord Jesus Christ; what was I, that I could

withstand God? When they heard these things, they held their peace, and glorified God, saying, Then hath God also to the Gentiles granted repentance unto life" (11:15-18).

This contrast may be observed between the experience in chapter 8 and in chapters 10 and 11. In chapter 8, the descent of the Holy Spirit was associated with the prayer of the Apostles and the laying on of hands by the Apostles. In chapter 10, in reference to the Gentiles, there was no prayer for the Holy Spirit to be sent, and there was no laying on of hands. God operated in two different ways, in these two experiences, to show us that this coming of the Holy Spirit was not directly attributable to the prayer of the Apostles or the position of the hands of the Apostles, but was the sovereign work of God, and God would work as it pleased Him. It was not that the Apostles had the right to order God as to what He should do. God sovereignly would bring into the body of Christ all those, whether Jew or Gentile, who had received Him as a personal Saviour.

There is yet another incident concerning the descent of the Holy Spirit. It takes us out of the land of Palestine and into Asia Minor. Paul, in his missionary journeys, has been going throughout that part of the earth proclaiming the gospel of salvation through the shed blood of Jesus Christ. As he came into the important city of Ephesus, he found certain disciples (Acts 19:1). They were not disciples of the Lord Jesus Christ; they were disciples of John the Baptist. John the Baptist had begun his ministry some months before Christ's ministry began, and in those months had brought to himself multitudes throughout Jerusalem and Judea. John's disciples were missionaries and they carried the message of their master far beyond Palestine. They announced that men should repent and be baptized, for the kingdom of heaven was at hand. Some of John's disciples had made converts in the city of Ephesus, and when Paul found them he found a group anticipating the coming of Messiah. They were praying for the revelation of God's Son from heaven. The most natural place for Paul to go was to those whose hearts were hungry; who were calling to God for a Deliverer and a Saviour. He did not have to convince these men that they needed salvation; he simply had to tell them that the Saviour they were expecting had made His appearance. So he said to them, "Have ye received the Holy Ghost since ye believed?" (Acts 19:2). His words have caused more problems in reference to the teaching on the second work of grace than perhaps any other passage in the New Testament. This passage is frequently read: "Have ye received the Holy Ghost *subsequent* to the time that ye believed?" And it would be possible, on the basis of this English translation, so to interpret it. If you would study this in the original text, you would find that the Apostle literally says, "Have ye received the Holy Ghost, having believed?" Or, if we were to interpret the original text, we would read it this way: "Did ye receive the Holy Spirit *when* ye believed?" or "Did you receive the Holy Spirit because ye are believers?" The Apostle is assuming faith and he is testing them concerning the Holy Spirit so as to discover the object of their faith. If they are believers in the Lord Jesus Christ, they will have received the Holy Spirit. So the question is a logical one, "Can you produce the evidence of your salvation? Namely, are you conscious of the presence of the Holy Spirit within you?" Romans 8:9 teaches: ". . . if any man have not the Spirit of Christ, he is none of his." "And they said unto him, We have not so much as heard whether there be any Holy Ghost" (Acts 19:2). If they were ignorant of the doctrine of the Person and work of the Holy Spirit, if they had no knowledge of the Spirit's indwelling presence, it must be because they had not been brought into the truths concerning the Lord Jesus Christ. They were still resting on the truths, the initial, introductory, truths that John proclaimed, and perhaps they had never experienced the fact of the new birth. Paul said to them, "Unto what then were ye baptized? And they said, Unto John's baptism" (v. 3). That explains their ignorance. John said nothing about receiving the Holy Spirit when they received his message; he prophesied the coming of the baptism of the Holy Spirit, but he could not bring about such a baptism. Then said Paul, "John verily baptized with the baptism of repentance, saying unto the people, that they should believe on him that should come after him, that is, on Christ Jesus. When they heard this, they were baptized in the name of the Lord Jesus" (vv. 4-5). Now, what had to precede this baptism? Obviously, faith. Paul presented the message that they should believe on Jesus Christ, and after they received Him they publicly witnessed it by baptism. And when Paul laid his hands on them, the Holy Ghost came upon them and they spoke with tongues and prophesied. This was not a *second* work of grace; it was that which accompanied their salvation. The very moment that they believed, and the hands of the Apostle were imposed upon them, the Holy Spirit came to dwell within them. Once again, the authority of the Apostle was used to bring them into a practical experience of relationship to the Holy Spirit.

After the initial act of the coming of the Holy Spirit for Jews, and the initial act of the coming of the Holy Spirit for Samaritans, and the initial act concerning Gentiles, both in Palestine and outside Palestine, there is no further record given of the coming of the Holy Spirit in response to the prayers of apostles. What I am emphasizing is the fact that when the transition has been made, and God has authenticated before men, by signs and wonders, that a particular group had been included within His plan, the signs and wonders cease. The Holy Spirit *had* come on the day of Pentecost. The Holy Spirit *had* taken up residence in the believer the very moment he believed. And as far as the great bodies of peoples are concerned, there was no need to repeat these actions, for God had signified that the body was to be made up of Jews, of Samaritans, and of Gentiles, all in fulfillment of the plan of the progress of the gospel as given to us in Acts 1.

We want to make several observations concerning this so-called second work of grace. As we have examined these Scriptures, we have seen that these acts of receiving the Holy Spirit were associated with believing and trusting Christ as personal Saviour. In the Book of Acts the manifestations of the Holy Spirit and the coming of the Holy Spirit to indwell the body, in each instance, were associated with believing and related to salvation. They were not related to progressive or experimental sanctification. In no case in the Book of Acts did this coming of the Holy Spirit depend on the sanctification of the individual. The failure to observe that fact is one of the most common fallacies in the so-called "second-work-of-grace" movement. They would teach us that one has to be sanctified, or made holy or righteous in his conduct to warrant the reception of the Holy Spirit as a reward for his righteousness or holiness. The coming of the Spirit was associated with salvation, not progressive sanctification.

It is necessary to distinguish between the *gift* of the Spirit and the *gifts* of the Spirit. Go back for a moment to Acts 10:45: "they of the circumcision which believed were astonished, as many as came with Peter, because that on the Gentiles also was poured out the gift [singular] of the Holy

Ghost." Also, in Acts 11:17: "Forasmuch then as God gave them the like *gift* as he did unto us, who believed on the Lord Jesus Christ; what was I, that I could withstand God." In these two instances, the gift of the Holy Spirit is the indwelling of the Holy Spirit, that sovereign work whereby the Holy Spirit of God comes to take up residence in the life of the believer the moment he accepts Jesus Christ as a personal Saviour. The *gift* of the Holy Spirit was given to Jews, to Samaritans, to Gentiles.

In I Corinthians 12:1, as we have seen in two previous studies, we read: "concerning spiritual gifts [plural], brethren, I would not have you ignorant." Again, in verse 4: "there are diversities of gifts. . . ." Admittedly, the giving of *gifts* by the Spirit may be subsequent to the time of salvation. One may be saved for a long time before he knows what his spiritual gift is, or before he begins to exercise his gift. The failure to observe the difference between the gift of the Spirit and the gifts of the Spirit has led many to believe that the gift of the Spirit comes at some subsequent time because the gifts of the Spirit come, or are realized, at some subsequent time.

Another fallacy in the "second-work-of-grace" movement arises out of the failure to observe the teaching given to us in Ephesians 1:3: "Blessed be the God and Father of our Lord Jesus Christ, who hath blessed us with all spiritual blessings in heavenly places in Christ." These blessings are outlined in the verses that follow. It is the teaching of the Apostle Paul in Ephesians 1 that every child of God has *every* blessing that an infinite God could devise to give to His children from the moment that they accept Jesus Christ as personal Saviour. The second-work-of-grace teaching says, "No, that is not true. God has some gifts for believers when they accept Christ as Saviour, and He has a special gift for a special few which will be received much later in their Christian experience." The teaching on a second work of grace denies the statement of the Apostle that every child of God has been blessed, not with most spiritual blessings, not with all spiritual blessings save one—the blessing of the Holy Spirit—but the child of God has been given and has received, from the moment that he has been born into the family of God, every conceivable blessing that an infinite God could devise.

If this second work of grace comes because we hunger for it, because we pray for it, because we shed tears for it, because we tarry at the altar to get it, it is in effect saying that God is unwilling to release the gift we seek; and that it is only as we pry loose the tightly clenched fingers of God that hold this gift to Himself that we possibly can get it. To say that this gift is to be sought by men is to say that God is unwilling to give His choicest blessing unless we force it out of Him. The Apostle emphasizes that God, in grace, withholds absolutely nothing.

The teaching is very clear in Romans 8:9, as the Apostle says, ". . . if any man have not the Spirit of Christ, he is none of his." If it is true that there is a second work of grace, then, according to the Word of God, one is not saved from the time he accepts Christ as Saviour until he gets the Holy Spirit at the second work of grace. For if a person does not have the Holy Spirit, he doesn't belong to Christ at all. In the light of this teaching you would have to count salvation from the moment of the second work of grace, not from the time of placing faith in the Lord Jesus Christ.

There is a principle stated for us in the Gospel of John that ought to settle this question. The Lord Jesus had been revealing the truth of God to one whose heart was hungry to know Him. He revealed the truth of the way into God's presence: "For God so loved the world, that he gave his only begotten Son, that whosoever believeth in him should not perish, but have everlasting life" (John 3:16). And the question logically arises, Since Christ has revealed truth, is it authoritative and trustworthy? John shows us how we can know that the revelation of the way of access to God, made by Jesus Christ, is trustworthy (3:31-36). He points out the fact that Jesus Christ has testified to what He has known; He has told us what He has seen and heard, and that His testimony is trustworthy. John adds, ". . . he whom God hath sent speaketh the words of God: for God giveth not the Spirit by measure *unto him*" (v. 34). You will observe that the last two words of that verse are in italics. "God does not give the Spirit by measure." John is affirming the truth that Jesus Christ could not reveal a lie to us because He has been ministering by the power of the Spirit, and when God gives the Spirit to one, He gives the Spirit fully. God does not dribble out the Spirit so that we have a little bit of Him now, and a little bit of Him again, and finally will come to the place of sanctification so that we can get the second blessing. The Word of God says, "God giveth not the Spirit by measure." The believer will not receive part at the time of salvation, and the rest later.

The greatest fallacy in this teaching on the second work of grace arises out of the failure to distinguish between the filling of the Spirit and the indwelling of the Spirit. In I Corinthians 6:19 the Apostle Paul questions: "What? know ye not that your body is the temple of the Holy Ghost. . . ?" He is writing to believers who are immature, ignorant, marked by secret and open sins, and yet the Apostle says their body is the temple of the Holy Ghost. In our previous study of the indwelling ministry of the Spirit we saw that the Word of God teaches that the Holy Spirit comes to take up residence in the body of the child of God the moment that he is born into the family of God. The believer becomes a temple; he becomes a part of the body of Christ of which the Lord Jesus Christ is the head. That indwelling ministry is universal: every child of God is indwelt.

On the other hand, the filling of the Holy Spirit is related to the believer's daily walk. When one is filled by the Holy Spirit, he is controlled by the Holy Spirit. One can be indwelt by the Spirit of God only once, but each day thereafter can bring a new submission to the control by the Spirit of God, and hence a new filling. There is need, every day, to reaffirm the truth that one is in the Lord's hands to do His will, and that He has the right to do with him as He pleases. The Apostle tells us that He will, once and for all, indwell; but that daily, hourly, momentarily, as we keep on submitting to control by the Holy Spirit of God, we are being kept filled. And because we daily must present our bodies to the Lord Jesus Christ for His use and submit to the control by the Spirit of God, many have falsely inferred that it is not until we submit that we will be indwelt by the Holy Spirit of God.

The believer will never have more of the Holy Spirit than he has the instant he accepts Jesus Christ as personal Saviour. Our problem, day by day, is not getting more of the Spirit, but letting the Spirit have all that there is of us. We rest by faith in the promise of God that He gives the Holy Spirit to indwell His children. We today are not seeking a second work of grace, as though God grudgingly had withheld some blessing from us. We thank God that we have all that He has to offer.

INDEX TO SCRIPTURES

INDEX

CPSIA information can be obtained
at www.ICGtesting.com
Printed in the USA
BVHW01s0155250118
506258BV00004B/17/P